Understanding System.IO for .NET Core 3

Implementing Internal and Commercial Tools

Roger Villela

Apress®

Understanding System.IO for .NET Core 3: Implementing Internal and Commercial Tools

Roger Villela
São Paulo, São Paulo, Brazil

ISBN-13 (pbk): 978-1-4842-5871-2   ISBN-13 (electronic): 978-1-4842-5872-9
https://doi.org/10.1007/978-1-4842-5872-9

Managing Director, Apress Media LLC: Welmoed Spahr
Acquisitions Editor: Smriti Srivastava
Development Editor: Matthew Moodie
Coordinating Editor: Shrikant Vishwakarma

Cover designed by eStudioCalamar

Cover image designed by Freepik (www.freepik.com)

Distributed to the book trade worldwide by Springer Science+Business Media New York, 233 Spring Street, 6th Floor, New York, NY 10013. Phone 1-800-SPRINGER, fax (201) 348-4505, e-mail orders-ny@springer-sbm.com, or visit www.springeronline.com. Apress Media, LLC is a California LLC and the sole member (owner) is Springer Science + Business Media Finance Inc (SSBM Finance Inc). SSBM Finance Inc is a **Delaware** corporation.

For information on translations, please e-mail rights@apress.com, or visit www.apress.com/rights-permissions.

Apress titles may be purchased in bulk for academic, corporate, or promotional use. eBook versions and licenses are also available for most titles. For more information, reference our Print and eBook Bulk Sales web page at www.apress.com/bulk-sales.

Any source code or other supplementary material referenced by the author in this book is available to readers on GitHub via the book's product page, located at www.apress.com/978-1-4842-5871-2. For more detailed information, please visit www.apress.com/source-code.

Printed on acid-free paper

This book is dedicated to my mother,

Marina Roel de Oliveira (†)
January 14, 1952 to March 17, 2017 (†)

Table of Contents

About the Author vii

About the Technical Reviewer ix

Acknowledgments xi

Introduction xiii

Chapter 1: About .NET Core 1
  Acronyms 1
  .NET Core Platform 2
  Target Framework Moniker 5
  Creating the RVJ.IO Library for .NET Core Using Microsoft Visual Studio 2019 8
  Summary 22
    Dos 23
    Don'ts 24

Chapter 2: Overview of Architecture for Implementation 25
  RVJ.IO Custom Library and the Architecture for Implementation 25
    Encapsulating Data Types 33
    Summary 52
    Dos 52
    Don'ts 54

Chapter 3: Custom Data Types for a Custom Library 57
  Purpose of Custom Data Types 57
  Working with Custom Data Types for Stream Data Types 66

Using C++/CLI Projection and .NET Core 73

Summary 77

　　Dos 77

　　Don'ts 78

Chapter 4: Custom Collections for a Custom Library 79

Overview 79

Fundamental Set of .NET Data Types for Collections in BCL 80

　　Non-Generic–Based Custom Collections 80

　　Generic-Based Custom Collections 86

　　Iteration Over Collections 94

Iteration Over a Collection, the Enumerator Pattern 107

　　The Engineering About for…each and Collections 113

Summary 122

　　Dos 122

　　Don't 122

Chapter 5: Custom Collections - About C++ Templates and .NET Generics 123

Working with C++ Templates – Welcome, Everyone 124

Templates and Encapsulating Knowledge 124

Fundamental Data Types 128

The Idea of a Template in Software Development Activities 133

Chapter 6: Unmanaged .NET Data Types and System.IO 153

Unmanaged .NET Data Types and System.IO 153

System.IO.UnmanagedMemoryStream .NET Data Type As an Example 162

Index 171

About the Author

 **Roger Villela** is a software engineer and entrepreneur with almost 30 years of experience in the industry. He works as an independent professional. Currently, he is focused on his work as a book author and technical educator. He specializes in the inner works of orthogonal features of the following Microsoft development platforms:

- Microsoft Windows base services

- Microsoft Universal Windows Platform (UWP)

- Microsoft WinRT

- Microsoft .NET Framework implementation of the runtime environment (CLR)

His work is based on Microsoft Visual Studio (Microsoft Windows) using the following programming languages, extensions, and projections:

- C/C++

- Assembly (Intel IA-32/Intel 64 (x64/amd64))

- Component extensions for runtimes (C++/CLI and C++/CX)

About the Technical Reviewer

 **Carsten Thomsen** is primarily a back-end developer, but he works with smaller front-end bits as well. He has authored and reviewed a number of books and created numerous Microsoft Learning courses, all to do with software development. He works as a freelancer/contractor in various countries in Europe using Azure, Visual Studio, Azure DevOps, and GitHub. among other tools. He's an exceptional troubleshooter and is adept at asking the right questions, including the less logical ones, in a most-logical-to-least-logical fashion. He also enjoys architecture, research, analysis, development, testing, and bug fixing. Carsten is a very good communicator with great mentoring and team-lead skills; he also has great skills in researching and presenting new material.

Acknowledgments

First, I would like to thank the people on the Apress team who worked with me on this book: Smriti Srivastava (Acquisitions Editor), Shrikant Vishwakarma (Coordinating Editor), Matthew Moodie (Development Editor), Welmoed Spahr (Managing Director), and Carsten Thomsen (Technical Reviewer). It was a pleasure and an honor work with such a highly professional team.

Thanks to my parents and a special thanks to my dad, Gilberto, and my two brothers, Eder and Marlos, and my sister-in-law Janaína, and my nephew Gabriel, and my nieces Lívia and Rafaela.

Special thanks to my cousin Ariadne Villela.

I would also like to thank my professional colleagues and friends who worked with me through these years.

Introduction

Working with software engineering is a challenge and a pleasure.

This book shows the reader how to take full advantage of the .NET APIs in System.IO in order to achieve fundamental I/O operations and produce better quality software.

The book starts with the basics of creating a .NET Core custom library for System.IO. You will learn the purpose and benefits of a custom cross-platform .NET Core library along with the implementation architecture of the custom library components. Moving forward, you will learn how to use the .NET APIs of System.IO for getting information about resources. Here, you will go through drives, directories, files, and much more in the .NET API. Manipulation of resources and environment is discussed, and you will learn how to build custom I/O actions for resource manipulation followed by its properties and security. Next, you will learn special .NET APIs operations with System.IO via demonstrations of working with a collection of resources, directories, files, and system information. Towards the end, you will go through the managed and unmanaged streams in the .NET API such as the memory stream, file stream, and much more.

After reading the book, you will be able to work with different features of System.IO in .NET Core and implement its internal and commercial tools to be used for different scenarios of I/O tasks.

INTRODUCTION

The Common Language Runtime (CLR), foundational libraries, and specialized libraries are organized in various components and technologies that use resources and features of System.IO .NET data types, and the coordination presents many challenges to the managed execution environment. The C# programming language is used to show important aspects of the behaviors of the resources and features of System. IO libraries, and it should be considered as part of your day-by-day too, as engineering practices.

CHAPTER 1

About .NET Core

In this chapter, you will get an overview of .NET Core and projects for the platform.

Acronyms

These acronyms will be introduced in this chapter:

- Application programming interface (API)

- Base Class Library (BCL)

- Common Type System (CTS)

- Common Intermediate Language (CIL)

- Common Language Infrastructure (CLI)

- Common Language Runtime (CLR)

- Common Language Specification (CLS)

- Framework Class Library (FCL)

- General availability (GA)

- Intermediate language (IL)

- Just-in-time (JIT)

- Target Framework Moniker (TFM)

© Roger Villela 2020
R. Villela, *Understanding System.IO for .NET Core 3*,
https://doi.org/10.1007/978-1-4842-5872-9_1

- Long-term support (LTS)

- Microsoft Intermediate Language (MSIL)

- Virtual Execution System (VES)

.NET Core Platform

.NET Core is an open source project that implements the ECMA-335 international standard specification and can also implement non-standard extensions provided by companies, institutions, and individuals. The .NET Full Framework implementation is also based on the ECMA-335 international standard specification.

The .NET Core open source project is maintained by Microsoft and by the .NET community, and the implementation is a self-contained .NET runtime and framework that is a cross-platform, general-purpose development platform providing support for, at least, Microsoft Windows, Apple macOS, and Linux distributions and/or derivations.

With the .NET Core platform, it is possible to write applications, libraries, and components for desktop development, web development, cloud development, device development, and IoT applications, for example.

The repositories of the open source projects are available on GitHub and organized by functionalities and contexts of the .NET Core platform.

The following is a short description captured from the repository with a list of the official main repositories of the .NET Core project itself and of the fundamental components of the runtime, such as the virtual execution environment and garbage collector mechanisms:

- GitHub repository for .NET Core (https://github.com/
  dotnet/core): .NET Core is a self-contained .NET runtime
  and framework that implements ECMA 335. It can be (and
  has been) ported to multiple architectures and platforms.
  It supports a variety of installation options, having no

specific deployment requirements itself. This repo includes several documents that explain both high-level and low-level concepts about the .NET runtime. They are particularly useful for contributors to get context that can be difficult to acquire from just reading code.

- GitHub repository for the .NET Core Runtime, the Core CLR (https://github.com/dotnet/coreclr): This is the runtime for .NET Core. It is composed of a garbage collector, JIT compiler, primitive data types, and low-level classes. The .NET Core Runtime implements the ECMA-335 specification, is a self-contained .NET runtime and framework, has been ported to multiple architectures and platforms, and, having no specific deployment requirements itself, supports a variety of installation options.

Here is the GitHub repository for the .NET Foundational Class Libraries, the BCL and FCL:

- GitHub repository for .NET Core Foundational Class Libraries, the BCL and FCL (https://github.com/dotnet/corefx): The .NET platform has a standard set of class libraries. The BCL (core set) is expected with any .NET implementation, because without it, we do not have a functional implementation of .NET. The FCL (complete set) is not fully required, but these two libraries provide .NET types for many general and app-specific types. Commercial and community libraries can be developed on top of the BCL and FCL libraries. The CoreFX repository contains both the BCL and the FCL.

For web development, cloud development, back-end services, and integration with IoT and mobile applications, there is also the official repository for the ASP.NET Core platform:

- GitHub repository for ASP.NET Core (`https://github.com/aspnet/AspNetCore`): ASP.NET Core is also an open-source, cross-platform framework for building web applications, cloud-based applications, IoT applications, and back-end services for mobile applications. It can be hosted on Windows, Mac, or Linux, and can be deployed in the cloud or on-premises.

The .NET Core platform can also be used to develop a redesigned implementation of technologies that are made for a specific platform such Microsoft .NET Windows Forms and Microsoft .NET WPF for the Microsoft Windows family of operating systems.

Here are the GitHub repositories of Microsoft .NET WPF and Microsoft .NET Windows Forms that now are officially .NET Core-based UI frameworks:

- GitHub repository for .NET WPF UI Framework (`https://github.com/dotnet/wpf`): The WPF is now officially a .NET Core-based UI framework for development of applications and components for Microsoft Windows Desktop. It runs exclusively on Microsoft Windows family of operating systems. It relies on Microsoft DirectX technologies, has a vector-based graphics architecture which enables the use of high-DPI monitors and infinity scale, and uses the Extensible Application Markup Language (XAML) to provide a declarative model for application programming.

- GitHub repository for .NET Core Windows Forms UI Framework (https://github.com/dotnet/winforms): The Windows Forms is now officially a .NET Core-based UI framework for developing applications and components for Microsoft Windows Desktop. The Windows Forms UI Framework runs exclusively on the Microsoft Windows family of operating systems and relies on Microsoft Windows GDI+ technology.

Target Framework Moniker

To specify one or more target frameworks of an application or library, you must use a standardized token format, the *Target Framework Moniker*.

At the time of this writing, here is the listing of TFMs currently supported by the Microsoft Visual Studio XML-based project file format and application configuration files for .NET:

- **.NET Standard:**
  - netstandard1.0
  - netstandard1.1
  - netstandard1.2
  - netstandard1.3
  - netstandard1.4
  - netstandard1.5
  - netstandard1.6
  - netstandard2.0
  - netstandard2.1

- **.NET Core:**
  - netcoreapp1.0
  - netcoreapp1.1
  - netcoreapp2.0
  - netcoreapp2.1
  - netcoreapp2.2
  - netcoreapp3.0
  - netcoreapp3.1
- **.NET Framework:**
  - net11
  - net20
  - net35
  - net40
  - net403
  - net45
  - net451
  - net452
  - net46
  - net461
  - net462
  - net47
  - net471
  - net472
  - net48

- **Universal Windows Platform:**

    - uap (instead of uap10.0).

    - uap10.0 (instead of win10 or netcore50).

For .NET Core, Microsoft officially released the .NET Core 3.1 GA LTS in November of 2019. The company is reorganizing Microsoft .NET and by the 2020 there will be only one .NET, and no more .NET Framework and .NET Core. You can read more at `https://devblogs.microsoft.com/dotnet/introducing-net-5/`.

According to an officially chronogram, Microsoft has the following releases scheduled:

- The new .NET 5.0 (GA) for November of 2020

- .NET 6.0 (LTS) for November of 2021

- .NET 7.0 (GA) for November of 2022

- .NET 8.0 (LTS) for November of 2023

When you are developing a library or code base that should be used as the starting point for more advanced software libraries and code bases, you must be aware of certain details for your projects and source code. The Target Framework Moniker is one of these details.

With the Microsoft Visual Studio Project's XML-based file format, you have a specific XML configuration tag and an object type available with the Microsoft Visual Studio Object Model for programming with this property.

The `<TargetFramework>` `</TargetFramework>` tag is used for configuring the Microsoft Visual Studio project for the main supported version of .NET Core. For the examples in this book, you'll use .NET Core version 3.1, as shown in Listing 1-1.

Listing 1-1. Excerpt of the Content of the Sample .csproj project File with the TargetFramework Property Configured for .Net Core Version 3.1

```
<Project Sdk="Microsoft.NET.Sdk">

  <PropertyGroup>
    <TargetFramework>netcoreapp3.1</TargetFramework>
  </PropertyGroup>

  <PropertyGroup Condition="'$(Configuration)|$(Platform)'==
  'Debug|AnyCPU'">
    <DefineConstants>DEBUG;TRACE</DefineConstants>
  </PropertyGroup>

</Project>
```

For example, in a configuration file of a .NET application or library, every time you set a version of the .NET platform, .NET Core, or .NET Framework, you use one of the standardized tokens for a TFM.

Now let's start writing the base structure for the sample RVJ.IO .NET Core library based on .NET Core 3.1 using the features and facilities of Microsoft Visual Studio 2019 for .NET Core in the next section.

Creating the RVJ.IO Library for .NET Core Using Microsoft Visual Studio 2019

Microsoft offers great support for the development of .NET Core from the Microsoft Visual Studio IDE. The images and comments in this section are based on features of Microsoft Visual Studio 2019 (Community, Professional, Enterprise) version 16.5.0 and .NET Core 3.1 GA LTS.

At the time of this writing, for Microsoft Visual Studio Enterprise 2019, these are the typical project templates for .NET Core and .NET Standard:

- Container Application for Kubernetes (C#, Azure)

- Console App (C#, F#, Visual Basic, Linux, macOS, Windows)

- ASP.NET Core Web Application (C#, F#, Linux, macOS, Windows)

- Blazor App (C#, Linux, macOS, Windows)

- Class Library (.NET Standard) (C#, F#, Visual Basic, Android, iOS, Linux, macOS, Windows)

- gRPC Service (C#, Linux, macOS, Windows)

- Razor Class Library (C#, Linux, macOS, Windows)

- Worker Service (C#, Linux, macOS, Windows)

- MSTest Test Project (C#, F#, Visual Basic, Linux, macOS, Windows)

- NUnit Test Project (C#, F#, Visual Basic, Linux, macOS, Windows)

- WPF App (C#, Windows)

- WPF Custom Control Library (C#, Windows)

- WPF User Control Library (C#, Windows)

- Windows Forms App (C#, Windows)

- Class Library (.NET Core) (C#, F#, Visual Basic, Linux, macOS, Windows)

- xUnit Test Project (C#, F#, Visual Basic, Linux, macOS, Windows)

- Web Driver Test for Edge (C#, Windows)

- Code Refactoring (.NET Standard) (C#, Visual Basic, Linux, macOS, Windows)

- Analyzer with Code Fix (.NET Standard) (C#, Visual Basic, Linux, macOS, Windows)

- Stand-Alone Code Analysis Tool (C#, Visual Basic, Linux, macOS, Windows)

- CLR Empty Project (C++, C++/CLI, Windows)

- CLR Class Library (C++, C++/CLI, Windows)

Figure 1-1 shows the Start window with some project templates listed in the center, filtered by the C# programming language and Library as the project type. It shows the listed template projects for .NET Standard, .NET Core, .NET Framework, and UWP such as Class Library and WPF Custom Control, for example.

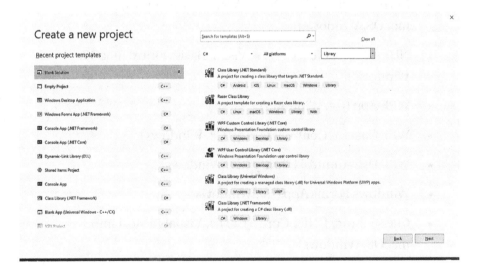

Figure 1-1. *Microsoft Visual Studio 2019 Start window showing the list of project templates*

Figure 1-2 shows the Start window with the Class Library (.NET Core) template project selected for the sample project's RVJ.IO custom class library.

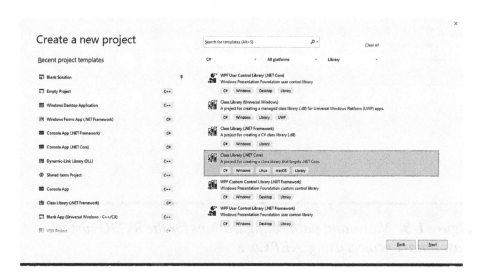

Figure 1-2. *Class Library (.NET Core) template project selected for the project's RVJ.IO custom class library*

In the companion source for this book, the sample project can be opened from the path `<install_folder>\Projects\RVJ\Books\CLR\System.IO\Ch01\`. Figure 1-3 shows an example of the name and path configurations for the RVJ.IO custom class library project using .NET Core.

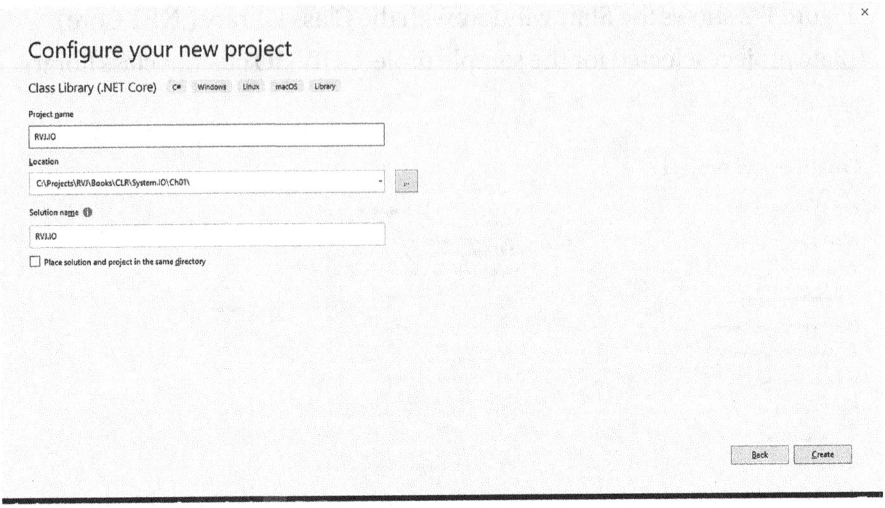

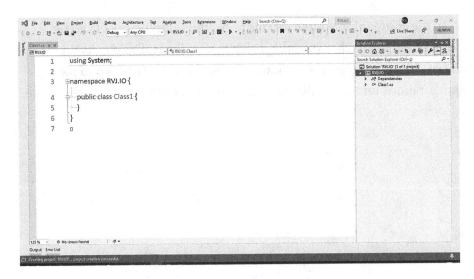

Figure 1-3. *Name and path configurations for the RVJ.IO custom class library project using .NET Core*

Figure 1-4 shows the RVJ.IO custom class library project using .NET Core, created and shown in the environment of Microsoft Visual Studio 2019.

Figure 1-4. *The RVJ.IO custom class library project, created and shown in Microsoft Visual Studio 2019*

In the Debug tab, you can check the box for Enable native code debugging, as shown in Figure 1-5.

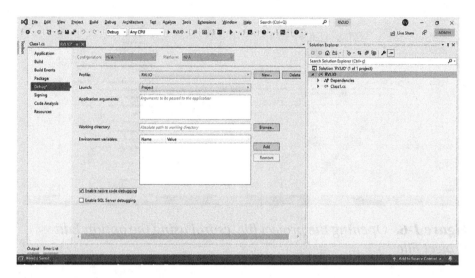

Figure 1-5. *Check the project property Enable native code debugging in the Debug tab*

Now, with some configuration changes, you can check the XML for the `.csproj` project file of Microsoft Visual Studio. You should have the fundamental configurations represented via an XML tag and with one or more values, as shown in Figures 1-6 and 1-7, and Listing 1-2.

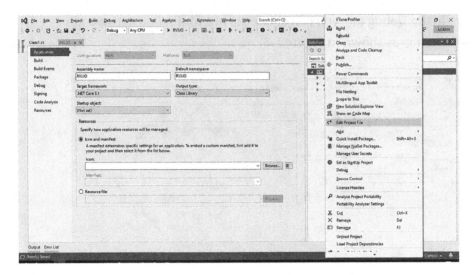

Figure 1-6. *Opening the project file .csproj using the option Edit Project File*

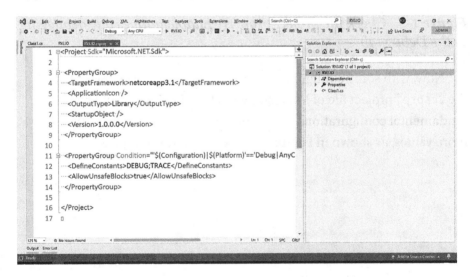

Figure 1-7. *The XML tags with configuration values for the options in the sample project*

Listing 1-2. XML Tags in .csproj with the Configured Option Values for the Sample Project

```
<Project Sdk="Microsoft.NET.Sdk">

  <PropertyGroup>
    <TargetFramework>netcoreapp3.1</TargetFramework>
    <ApplicationIcon />
    <OutputType>Library</OutputType>
    <StartupObject />
    <Version>1.0.0.0</Version>
  </PropertyGroup>

  <PropertyGroup Condition="'$(Configuration)|$(Platform)'==
    'Debug|AnyCPU'">
    <DefineConstants>DEBUG;TRACE</DefineConstants>
    <AllowUnsafeBlocks>true</AllowUnsafeBlocks>
  </PropertyGroup>

</Project>
```

Your .NET Core or .NET Framework applications and libraries can also target a version of .NET Standard, which are standardized sets of APIs that work across all .NET implementations. Using a library such as the RVJ.IO sample project, you can target a version of .NET Standard and gain access to APIs that work across .NET Core and .NET Framework using the same code base. In Listing 1-3, you change the RVJ.IO.csproj project file to use TFM for .NET Standard version 2.1. Note that the target framework in the project properties is also automatically changed, as shown in Figure 1-8.

Listing 1-3. Configuration File Using .NET Standard 2.1

```
<Project Sdk="Microsoft.NET.Sdk">

  <PropertyGroup>
<!--<TargetFramework>netcoreapp3.1</TargetFramework>-->

    <TargetFramework>netstandard2.1</TargetFramework>

    <ApplicationIcon />
    <OutputType>Library</OutputType>
    <StartupObject />
    <Version>1.0.0.0</Version>
  </PropertyGroup>

  <PropertyGroup Condition="'$(Configuration)|$(Platform)'==
   'Debug|AnyCPU'">
    <DefineConstants>DEBUG;TRACE</DefineConstants>
    <AllowUnsafeBlocks>true</AllowUnsafeBlocks>
  </PropertyGroup>

</Project>
```

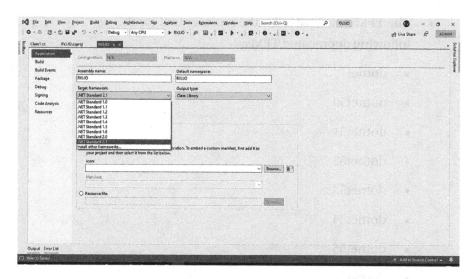

Figure 1-8. *The target framework on the project properties is also automatically changed to using the .NET Standard for your class library project*

You should be aware of deprecated TFMs that should be updated to the new TFMs. Here is a list of deprecated TFMs and the replacements:

- The TFM **netcoreapp** is the replacement for the following deprecated TFMs:

  - aspnet50

  - aspnetcore50

  - dnxcore50

  - dnx

  - dnx45

  - dnx451

  - dnx452

17

- The TFM **netstandard** is the replacement for the following deprecated TFMs:

    - dotnet

    - dotnet50

    - dotnet51

    - dotnet52

    - dotnet53

    - dotnet54

    - dotnet55

    - dotnet56

- The TFM **uap10.0** is the replacement for the following deprecated TFMs:

    - netcore50

    - win10

- The TFM **netcore45** is the replacement for the following deprecated TFMs:

    - win

    - win8

    - winrt

- The TFM **netcore451** is the replacement for the following deprecated TFM:

    - win81

If you are migrating or developing a .NET project that should support .NET Framework and .NET Core, you should use the `<TargetFrameworks>` `</TargetFrameworks>` tag (plural), instead of `<TargetFramework/>` tag (singular).

The use of `<TargetFrameworks></TargetFrameworks>` tag (plural) is also required if you are using multiple versions of the same framework for the same project, that is, .NET Framework or .NET Core.

Listing 1-4 contains the `RVJ.IO.csproj` sample project file using the `<TargetFrameworks></TargetFrameworks>` tag (plural) for supporting netcoreapp3.1 TFM and netstandard2.1 TFM.

Listing 1-4. Project File Supporting netcoreapp3.1 TFM and netstandard2.1 TFM Using the <TargetFrameworks> </TargetFrameworks> tag (plural)

```
<Project Sdk="Microsoft.NET.Sdk">

  <PropertyGroup>
<!--<TargetFramework>netcoreapp3.1</TargetFramework>-->
<!--<TargetFramework>netstandard2.1</TargetFramework>-->
<TargetFrameworks>netcoreapp3.1;netstandard2.1</
TargetFrameworks>

    <ApplicationIcon />
    <OutputType>Library</OutputType>
    <StartupObject />
    <Version>1.0.0.0</Version>
  </PropertyGroup>

  <PropertyGroup Condition="'$(Configuration)|$(Platform)'==
   'Debug|AnyCPU'">
    <DefineConstants>DEBUG;TRACE</DefineConstants>
    <AllowUnsafeBlocks>true</AllowUnsafeBlocks>
  </PropertyGroup>

</Project>
```

When supporting various target frameworks, you need to change your source code too because not every .NET type exists in every implementation of the target .NET library. So, you need to use preprocessor directives for conditional inclusion of blocks of source code depending on the configured target frameworks. Listing 1-5 contains the RVJ.IO source code with the conditional symbols for TFMs netcoreapp3.1 and netstandard2.1. At the time of this writing, this is the list with conditional symbols representing the TFMs:

- For the **.NET Framework**, the conditional symbols are

  - NETFRAMEWORK

  - NET20

  - NET35

  - NET40

  - NET45

  - NET451

  - NET452

  - NET46

  - NET461

  - NET462

  - NET47

  - NET471

  - NET472

  - NET48

- For the **.NET Core**, the conditional symbols are

  - NETCOREAPP

  - NETCOREAPP1_0

  - NETCOREAPP1_1

  - NETCOREAPP2_0

  - NETCOREAPP2_1

  - NETCOREAPP2_2

  - NETCOREAPP3_0

  - NETCOREAPP3_1

- For the **.NET Standard**, the conditional symbols are

  - netstandard

  - netstandard1_0

  - netstandard1_1

  - netstandard1_2

  - netstandard1_3

  - netstandard1_4

  - netstandard1_5

  - netstandard1_6

  - netstandard2_0

  - netstandard2_1

Listing 1-5. RVJ.IO Source Code with the Symbols for TFMs netcoreapp3.1 and netstandard2.1

```
using System;
#if DEBUG
using System.Diagnostics;
#endif

namespace RVJ.IO {
    public class Class1 {
        public Class1() {
#if NETCOREAPP3_1 || netstandard2_1

#if DEBUG
            Debug.WriteLine( "Using DEBUG symbol!" );
#endif

#endif


        }

    };
};
```

Summary

The next two sections offer recommendations about the use of characteristics of .NET Core.

Dos

- If a project needs the functionalities of specific .NET types, use .NET Framework until the functionalities that the project requires are available for .NET Core and .NET BCL/FCL Core.

- Be aware that the .NET Core runtime and infrastructure components of .NET Core are the bases for all Microsoft .NET investments from now on. This non-specific development platform is available for Microsoft Windows, Linux implementations, and the Apple macOS platform. This opens up new opportunities for application, library, and component developers.

- When necessary, work with a higher-level API for your code and consider APIs that abstract the details of a more specific operating system and low-level programming.

- If you are planning to migrate a big application such as an ERP or CRM to .NET Core, remember to establish business goals for multiplatform opportunities and do not focus only on the technical aspects.

- Use .NET Core 3.1 LTS to start any big migration to the .NET Core platform.

Don'ts

- Start a project using a version earlier than .NET Core 3.1 LTS. This is a Microsoft recommendation because previous versions are not supported for the long term. There are more features available, and it will facilitate the migration to .NET 5, which will be available in November of 2020 and will replace all previous versions of .NET Framework and .NET Core, including .NET Core 3.1.

- Consider any big migration to .NET Core until all of the functionalities that the project will be using are available for .NET Core and .NET BCL/FCL Core, especially Microsoft Windows Forms and Microsoft WPF.

- Define goals based on superficial technical observations about .NET Core. Instead, create pieces of software based on the required functionalities for your applications, libraries, and components, and make objective tests.

CHAPTER 2

Overview of Architecture for Implementation

In this chapter, I will talk about the architecture for implementing a custom library using .NET Core System.IO features.

RVJ.IO Custom Library and the Architecture for Implementation

The .NET Core platform can be used to develop a redesigned implementation of extraordinary technologies, and the RVJ.IO custom library has the architecture for implementation organized with the purpose of encapsulating and simplifying the use of resources available in .NET Core data types in BCL System.IO.* namespaces, via managed and unmanaged APIs.

At the time of this writing and for .NET Core version 3.1, the following namespaces are available for the System.IO.*:

- System.IO (root namespace)

- System.IO.Pipes

© Roger Villela 2020
R. Villela, *Understanding System.IO for .NET Core 3*,
https://doi.org/10.1007/978-1-4842-5872-9_2

- System.IO.Packaging

- System.IO.Enumeration

- System.IO.Compression

- System.IO.IsolatedStorage

- System.IO.MemoryMappedFiles

In this book, we will use the .NET Core data types available in the .NET Core BCL System.IO (root namespace) for the sample project RVJ.IO custom library .NET Core data types and demonstration for the model of the implementation, but the general concepts, ideas, and organizational distributions apply to the other namespaces of BCL System.IO.* when implemented.

Figure 2-1 shows a high-level view of the organizational architecture and distribution of responsibilities by technological contexts.

For example, Client Application One, Client Application Two, and Client Application "N" are typical .NET Core applications such as WPF, Windows Forms, Console, other .NET Core libraries, or any other .NET Core type application that can access the .NET Core System.IO resources encapsulated by the RVJ.IO custom library or any other .NET Core custom library.

The .NET Core RVJ.IO (custom library) context encapsulates the resources and functionalities of the .NET Core data types available in System.IO.* namespaces, managed data types, and unmanaged data types.

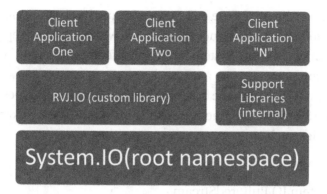

Figure 2-1. *Suggested architecture for implementation and distribution of responsibilities in technological contexts*

The context for the Support Libraries (internal) are more .NET Core projects or non-.NET Core projects that provide the support required by the resources encapsulated by the .NET Core RVJ.IO custom library. For example, if a .NET Core RVJ.IO custom library requires C/C++ source code for managing certain unmanaged resources for integrating the features into the .NET Core RVJ.IO custom library, these details are the responsibility of these internal support libraries.

The Client Applications context never directly access these internal support libraries. Only the .NET Core RVJ.IO custom library can access these internal custom libraries, directly or indirectly via other libraries.

Another important aspect is that not every resource or feature of the System.IO.* namespaces is available for .NET Core yet and will not be available for a while. Remember that System.IO.* was developed for the .NET Framework and some portions of the System.IO.* data types have been ported to .NET Core and work on multiple platforms, such as Microsoft Windows, Linux distributions, and Apple macOS, but other resources are made specifically to work with Microsoft Windows, or some other operating system for specific scenarios.

27

For example, the .NET Core BCL System.IO has the abstract concept of a data stream defined as a sequence of bytes, and we have the concept of a data stream implemented as the System.IO.Stream reference data type, that is an abstract reference type.

The System.IO.Stream is the base reference type for all .NET types of streams defined in the System.IO.* namespaces and other namespaces of other .NET Core assemblies, such as

- System.IO.FileStream

- System.IO.BufferedStream

- System.Data.OracleClient.OracleBFile

- System.Data.SqlTypes.SqlFileStream

At the time of this writing, System.Data.OracleClient.OracleBFile and System.Data.SqlTypes.SqlFileStream are not available yet for .NET Core, only for .NET Framework, but the documentation of the System.IO.Stream abstract reference type indicates a general view of some important derived reference types, not considering .NET Core or .NET Framework as a filter in the documentation, as you can see in Figure 2-2.

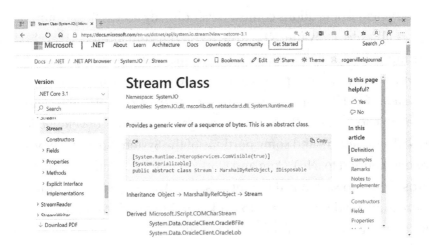

Figure 2-2. *Microsoft official documentation for the System. IO.Stream abstract reference type in .NET Core*

If you click the link for System.Data.OracleClient.OracleBFile or the link for System.Data.SqlTypes.SqlFileStream, you will see the documentation pages for both .NET data types with an alert at the top of the page saying that the current .NET type does not exist for .NET Core, as shown in Figures 2-3 and 2-4.

Some important .NET data types are available as extension packages via NuGet and can be implemented in future distributions of both .NET Framework and .NET Core. When planning the architecture for the implementation of custom libraries in general, you must consider these scenarios and include some programming logic in your source code base to deal with these scenarios.

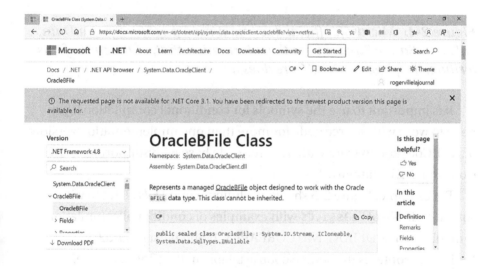

Figure 2-3. *Microsoft official documentation page for System.Data. OracleClient.OracleBFile with the information that, at the time of this writing, the page for .NET Core does not exists*

Figure 2-4. *Microsoft official documentation page for System.Data. SqlTypes.SqlFileStream with the information that, at the time of this writing, the page for .NET Core does not exist*

It is important to use the symbols for conditional compilation if you need to work with source code for more than one implementation version of .NET Core and to work with a source code base with support for .NET Core and .NET Framework.

For example, Figure 2-5 shows a solution named RVJ.IO.sln with a source code file of Class1.cs with examples of conditional compilation symbols such as DEBUG, NETCOREAPP3_1, and netstandard2_1. Listing 2-1 contains the source code available in the Class1.cs file.

Listing 2-1. Example of the Use of Conditional Compilation Symbols

```
using System;
#if DEBUG
using System.Diagnostics;
#endif
```

```
namespace RVJ.IO {
    public class Class1 {
        public Class1() {
#if NETCOREAPP3_1 || netstandard2_1

#if DEBUG

            Debug.WriteLine( "Using DEBUG symbol!" );
#endif

#endif


        }

    };
};
```

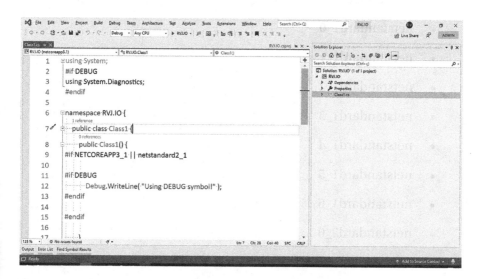

Figure 2-5. *Source code for Class1.cs using DEBUG, NETCOREAPP3_1, and netstandard2_1 conditional compilation symbols*

At the time of this writing, the **.NET Core** conditional symbols are

- NETCOREAPP
- NETCOREAPP1_0
- NETCOREAPP1_1
- NETCOREAPP2_0
- NETCOREAPP2_1
- NETCOREAPP2_2
- NETCOREAPP3_0
- NETCOREAPP3_1

At the time of this writing, the **.NET Standard** conditional symbols are

- netstandard
- netstandard1_0
- netstandard1_1
- netstandard1_2
- netstandard1_3
- netstandard1_4
- netstandard1_5
- netstandard1_6
- netstandard2_0
- netstandard2_1

At the time of this writing, the **.NET Framework** conditional symbols are

- NETFRAMEWORK
- NET20

- NET35

- NET40

- NET45

- NET451

- NET452

- NET46

- NET461

- NET462

- NET47

- NET471

- NET472

- NET48

Encapsulating Data Types

You should encapsulate .NET Core data types in BCL System.IO.*
namespaces such as .NET Core enumerations to avoid exposing any
specific kind of .NET Core data type in BCL System.IO.* directly through
your .NET Core RVJ.IO custom library programming interfaces.

This encapsulation via RVJ.IO custom data types helps, for example,

- protect the conceptual model of your custom library.

- manage updates of .NET Core BCL System.IO.* through
  your custom libraries.

- manage updates of the .NET Core infrastructure
  throughout your custom libraries APIs.

- update the management of your custom libraries APIs
  in future fixes, when necessary.

For example, in the System.IO namespace, you have common .NET Core enumerations that should be encapsulated in custom data types of your RVJ.IO custom library. Listing 2-2 shows some enumeration members of System.IO.DriveType encapsulated in a RVJ.IO.DriveType enumeration.

It is important to remember that you do not have to encapsulate every member of System.IO namespaces in a data type in RVJ.IO at the first moment. You must include custom data types that help your custom library and simplify the use of the .NET Core System.IO namespace data types encapsulated.

You must include a specific .NET Core System.IO data type as part of the encapsulated RVJ.IO custom data types by demand, and not just by doing a map one-by-one without a specific good technical reason or good business reason. For example, for the RVJ.IO.DriveType shown in Listing 2-2, not all members of the System.IO.DriveType enumeration are included; only the most common ones are.

Figure 2-6 shows a suggested set of data types of .NET Core System.IO as part of sample project RVJ.IO. This will be shown in more detail starting in Chapter 3.

Listing 2-2. Encapsulating Common Members of System.IO.DriveType

```
using System;
#if DEBUG
using System.Diagnostics;
#endif

namespace RVJ.IO {
    public enum DriveType {
        Fixed =   System.IO.DriveType.Fixed,
                  Ram = System.IO.DriveType.Ram,
```

```
        Network = System.IO.DriveType.Network,
        CDRom = System.IO.DriveType.CDRom,
        Removable = System.IO.DriveType.Removable
    };
};
```

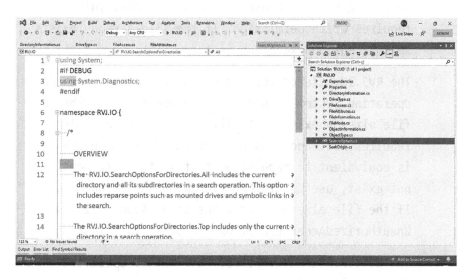

Figure 2-6. *Showing RVJ.IO examples of data types encapsulating functionalities of .NET Core data types of the BCL System.IO namespace*

Listing 2-3 shows the implementation of the RVJ.IO.FileMode .NET Core enumeration that encapsulates some members of the System. IO.FileMode .NET Core enumeration.

Listing 2-3. System.IO.FileMode Members Encapsulated by RVJ. IO.FileMode

```
using System;
#if DEBUG
using System.Diagnostics;
#endif
```

```
namespace RVJ.IO {

    /*

        OVERVIEW

        The RVJ.IO.FileMode.New method specifies that the
        operating system should create a new file. This
        requires write permission. If the file already exists,
        an IOException exception is thrown.

        The RVJ.IO.FileMode.Create method specifies that the
        operating system should create a new file. If the
        file already exists, it will be overwritten. This
        requires Write permission. System.IO.FileMode.Create
        is equivalent to requesting that if the file does
        not exist, use CreateNew; otherwise, use Truncate.
        If the file already exists but is a hidden file, an
        UnauthorizedAccessException exception is thrown.

        The RVJ.IO.FileMode.OpenOrCreate method specifies
        that the operating system should open a file if it
        exists; otherwise, a new file should be created. If the
        file is opened with System.IO.FileAccess.Read, Read
        permission is required. If the file access is System.
        IO.FileAccess.Write, Write permission is required. If
        the file is opened with System.IO.FileAccess.ReadWrite,
        both Read and Write permissions are required.

        The RVJ.IO.FileMode.Open Specifies that the operating
        system should open an existing file. The ability to
        open the file is dependent on the value specified by the
        System.IO.FileAccess enumeration. A FileNotFoundException
        exception is thrown if the file does not exist.
```

The RVJ.IO.FileMode.Append opens the file if it exists and seeks to the end of the file, or creates a new file. This requires Append permission. System. IO.FileMode.Append can be used only in conjunction with System.IO.FileAccess.Write. Trying to seek to a position before the end of the file throws an IOException exception, and any attempt to read fails and throws a NotSupportedException exception.

The RVJ.IO.FileMode.Truncate specifies that the operating system should open an existing file. When the file is opened, it should be truncated so that its size is zero bytes. This requires Write permission. Attempts to read from a file opened with System.IO.FileMode. Truncate causes an ArgumentException exception.

```
*/
public enum FileMode {
    New = System.IO.FileMode.CreateNew,
            Create = System.IO.FileMode.Create,
            OpenOrCreate = System.IO.FileMode.
            OpenOrCreate,
            Open = System.IO.FileMode.Open,
            Append = System.IO.FileMode.Append,
            Truncate = System.IO.FileMode.Truncate
    };
};
```

You can check the RVJ.IO custom library and see that you have more custom enumerations that encapsulate .NET Core System.IO enumerations and the same model for implementation is used.

But your .NET Core RVJ.IO custom library does not only encapsulate enumerations.

When you are developing a custom library or a code base that should be used as a starting point for more advanced software libraries and source code bases, you must be aware of certain details of your projects and source code.

Your RVJ.IO will encapsulate specialized behaviors of .NET Core data types available in the BCL System.IO namespace.

The .NET Core data types in System.IO.* namespaces do the management of the input and output of operations via some type of data stream.

You need an enumeration that identifies this type of data stream, and this is implemented in the source file StreamType.cs. Initially you have three types of data streams, as shown in Listing 2-4.

Listing 2-4. Types of Data Streams Defined in the Enumeration RVJ. IO.StreamType

```csharp
using System;
#if DEBUG
using System.Diagnostics;
#endif

namespace RVJ.IO {
    /*

        OVERVIEW

    */
    public  enum StreamType {
        Directory,
                    File,
                    Memory,
                    Unknown // The data stream is managed as a
                                pure sequence of bytes.
    };
};
```

When working with a data stream, one behavior that is necessary is to get information about the data stream, and this is implemented in source code file StreamInformation.cs, as shown in Listing 2-5.

The example shown in Listing 2-5 is just a suggestion with a sample implementation and organization with some fields, methods, and properties that can be useful for the management of information.

You can insert into this kind of data type some data stream information that is generic enough, but more specific for an operating system or technological contexts such as networks and databases.

Listing 2-5. Suggestion with Sample Source Code for an Implementation of the .NET Core Data Type StreamInformation

```
using System;
#if DEBUG
using System.Diagnostics;
#endif

namespace RVJ.IO {

    public sealed class StreamInformation : System.Object,
    RVJ.IO.IStreamInformation {

        #region Common Fields
        // Type of data stream.
        private StreamType _type;
        // Name of data stream (real of not).
        private String _name;
        // Size (32-bit) of data stream, if available. Can be
           zero or a negative value.
        private Int32 _sizeInBytes;
        // Larger size (64-bit) of a data stream, if available.
           Can be zero or a negative value.
        private Int64 _largerSizeInBytes;
```

```csharp
// Date of creation of data stream.
private DateTime _creationDateTime;
// Date of last update of data stream.
private DateTime _lastUpdateDateTime;
#endregion

#region Stream management typical fields
// The opened data stream of some specialized type.
private System.IO.Stream _dataStream;

// Type of operation, read/write/seek/all, that can be
   used with the data stream.
private StreamOperationType _operationType;

// Fields for working with the position when moving
   between bytes within the sequence.
private UInt32 _currentPosition32;
private UInt32 _nextPosition32;
private UInt32 _previousPosition32;
private UInt64 _lastPosition32; // Not the last byte
                                   in the data stream,
                                   but the last useful
                                   position for the
                                   application.
private UInt64 _currentPosition64;
private UInt64 _nextPosition64;
private UInt64 _previousPosition64;
private UInt64 _lastPosition64; // Not the last byte
                                   in the data stream,
                                   but the last useful
                                   position for the
                                   application.

// The sequence of bytes stored in an internal data
   stream.
```

```csharp
private Byte[] _internalStream;

#endregion

#region Constructors
public StreamInformation() : base() {

    this._type = StreamType.File;
    this._name = String.Empty;
    this._sizeInBytes = new Int32();
    this._largerSizeInBytes = new Int64();
    this._creationDateTime = DateTime.Now;
    this._lastUpdateDateTime = DateTime.Now;

    this._dataStream = null;
    this._operationType = StreamOperationType.None;

    this._currentPosition32 = new UInt32();
    this._nextPosition32 = new UInt32();
    this._previousPosition32 = new UInt32();
    this._lastPosition32 = new UInt32();
    this._currentPosition64 = new UInt64();
    this._nextPosition64 = new UInt64();
    this._previousPosition64 = new UInt64();
    this._lastPosition64 = new UInt64();

    this._internalStream = null;

    return;
}

public StreamInformation( StreamType type ) : this() {

    switch ( type ) {
        case StreamType.Directory:
        case StreamType.File:
        case StreamType.Memory: {
```

```
        };
        break;
        default: break;
    }

    return;
}
#endregion

#region Methods

/// <summary>
/// Verifies if the data stream was created.
/// </summary>
public Boolean Exists() {
    Boolean _exists = new Boolean();

    return _exists;
}

/// <summary>
///  Tries to open the data stream.
/// </summary>
public Boolean Open() {

    return new Boolean();
}

/// <summary>
/// Tries to read some portion of the data stream.
/// Returns the readed portion of data stream in  a
    System.Byte[] array.
```

```
/// </summary>
public Byte[] Read( OperationDirection
operationDirection, UInt32 numberOfBytes, Boolean
asyncOperation ) {

    Boolean _argumentValuesValid = new Boolean();
    UInt32 _localValue = new UInt32();

    switch ( operationDirection ) {
        case OperationDirection.Forward: {
            // The number of bytes must be greater
                than zero.
            _argumentValuesValid = ( numberOfBytes
             > _localValue );
        };
            break;
        case OperationDirection.Back: {
            // The number of bytes must be negative.
            _argumentValuesValid = ( numberOfBytes
            < _localValue );
        };
            break;
        default: // For the zero value, does nothing.
            break;
    }

    if ( asyncOperation ) {
        // Should use the async available methods for
            management of data stream.
    } else {
        // Should use the non-async available methods
            for management of data stream.
    };
```

```
        return this._internalStream;
    }

/// <summary>
/// Tries to write to the data stream.
/// </summary>
public Boolean Write( ) {

    Boolean _written = new Boolean();

    return _written;
}

/// <summary>
/// Tries to close the data stream.
/// </summary>
public Boolean Close() {

    Boolean _closed = new Boolean();

    return _closed;
}
#endregion

#region Public Properties
/// <summary>
/// Type of data stream.
/// </summary>
public StreamType Type {
    get {
        return this._type;
    }

    set {
```

```
            this._type = value;
            return;
        }
    }

    /// <summary>
    /// Name of data stream (real or virtual).
    /// </summary>
    public String Name {
        get {
            return this._name;
        }

        set {
            if ( !String.IsNullOrEmpty( value ) )
            this._name = value;
            return;
        }
    }

    /// <summary>
    /// Size of data stream (32-bit). Can be zero or a
        negative value.
    /// </summary>
    public Int32 SizeInBytes {

        get {
            return this._sizeInBytes;
        }

        set { this._sizeInBytes = value; return;  }

    }
```

```csharp
/// <summary>
/// Larger size (64-bit) of a data stream, if
    available. Can be zero or a negative value.
/// </summary>
public Int64 LargerSizeInBytes {
    get { return this._largerSizeInBytes; }
    set { this._largerSizeInBytes = value; return;  }
}

/// <summary>
/// Date of creation of data stream.
/// </summary>
public DateTime Creation {
    get { return this._creationDateTime; }
    set { this._creationDateTime = value; return;  }
}

/// <summary>
/// Date of last update of data stream.
/// </summary>
public DateTime LastUpdate {
    get { return this._lastUpdateDateTime; }
    set { this._lastUpdateDateTime = value; return;  }
}

/// <summary>
/// Indicates the type of operation supported by the
    data stream at this moment.

/// </summary>
public StreamOperationType OperatingType {
    get { return this._operationType; }
    set { this._operationType = value; return; }
}
```

```csharp
/// <summary>
/// Indicates if an operation of read can be realized.
/// </summary>
public Boolean CanRead {
    get { return this._operationType ==
    ( StreamOperationType.All | StreamOperationType.
    Read | StreamOperationType.Seek ); }
}

/// <summary>
/// Indicates if an operation of write can be realized.
/// </summary>
public Boolean CanWrite {
    get { return this._operationType ==
    ( RVJ.IO.StreamOperationType.All | RVJ.
    IO.StreamOperationType.Write ); }
}

public System.IO.Stream DataStream {
    get { return this._dataStream;  }
    set {  if ( value != null ) this._dataStream =
    value; return; }
}
#endregion
    };
};
```

The idea of the RVJ.IO.StreamInformation reference type is to have the common and most fundamental fields and behaviors for getting and storing information of an instance of a data stream.

The .NET Core data type RVJ.IO.StreamInformation is a reference type that can be used as the base class for other .NET data types that specialize in getting information about a specific data stream, such as System.IO.FileStream, System.IO.BufferedStream, System.IO.MemoryStream, or others.

But, as shown in Listing 2-5, the sample implementation has the `sealed` C# keyword, showing that another reference type cannot inherit from RVJ.IO.StreamInformation reference type, directly or indirectly.

The RVJ.IO.StreamInformation reference type is derived from System.Object and it implements the fundamental concepts of methods System.Object.Equals(), System.Object.ReferenceEquals(), System.Object.GetHashCode(), and System.Object.ToString(), for example.

The RVJ.IO.StreamInformation reference type implements the RVJ.IO.IStreamInformation interface that derives from the RVJ.IO.IStream interface that is the fundamental abstraction for the idea of a data stream that is part of the System.IO.* .NET Core libraries' implementations.

Listings 2-6 and 2-7 show the first suggestion of the RVJ.IO.IStream and RVJ.IO.IStreamInformation interfaces.

Listing 2-6. Suggestion for the RVJ.IO.IStream Interface

```
using System;
#if DEBUG
using System.Diagnostics;
#endif

namespace RVJ.IO {

    /*

        OVERVIEW

    */
    public interface IStream {
```

```
#region Behaviors
/// <summary>
///  Tries to open the data stream.
/// </summary>
Boolean Open();
/// <summary>
/// Verifies if the data stream was created.
/// </summary>
Boolean Exists();

/// <summary>
/// Tries to read some portion of the data stream.
/// Returns the readed portion of data stream
    in  System.Byte[] array.
/// </summary>
Byte[] Read( OperationDirection operationDirection,
UInt32 numberOfBytes, Boolean asyncOperation );

/// <summary>
/// Tries to write to the data stream.
/// </summary>
Boolean Write();

/// <summary>
/// Tries to close the data stream.
/// </summary>
Boolean Close();
#endregion

#region Properties
/// <summary>
/// Base data stream object instance that was opened
    for manipulation.
```

```
        /// </summary>
        System.IO.Stream DataStream { get; set; }
        #endregion

    };


};
```

Listing 2-7. Suggestion for the RVJ.IO.IStreamInformation Interface

```
using System;
#if DEBUG
using System.Diagnostics;
#endif

namespace RVJ.IO {
    /*

    OVERVIEW

*/
    public interface IStreamInformation : RVJ.IO.IStream {

        #region Properties
        /// <summary>
        /// Type of data stream.
        /// </summary>
        RVJ.IO.StreamType Type { get; set; }

        /// <summary>
        /// Name of data stream (real or virtual).
        /// </summary>
        String Name { get; set; }

        /// <summary>
```

```
/// Size of data stream (32-bit). Can be zero or a
    negative value.
/// </summary>
Int32 SizeInBytes { get; set; }

/// <summary>
/// Larger size (64-bit) of a data stream, if
    available. Can be zero or a negative value.
/// </summary>
Int64 LargerSizeInBytes { get; set; }

/// <summary>
/// Date of creation of data stream.
/// </summary>
DateTime Creation { get; set; }

/// <summary>
/// Date of last update of data stream.
/// </summary>
DateTime LastUpdate { get; set; }

/// <summary>
/// Indicates the type of operation supported by the
    data stream at this moment.
/// </summary>
RVJ.IO.StreamOperationType OperatingType { get; set; }

/// <summary>
/// Indicates if an operation of read can be realized.
/// </summary>
Boolean CanRead { get; }

/// <summary>
/// Indicates if an operation of write can be realized.
```

```
        /// </summary>
        Boolean CanWrite { get; }

        #endregion

    };
};
```

In Chapter 3, you will be working with details of the suggested organization of source code files and implementation for the RVJ.IO custom library and some code in the C++/CLI projection.

In Chapter 4, you will learn about unmanaged data types and the suggested use of them in your RVJ.IO custom library and the internal support libraries.

Summary

The next two sections offer recommendations about the uses of characteristics of .NET Core.

Dos

- Consider the use of the C++/CLI projection for the development of .NET Core custom libraries. Yes, C++/CLI supports the .NET Core as a target platform, which I will be talking about in Chapter 3 and throughout the book.

- The .NET Core platform can be used to develop a redesigned implementation of extraordinary technologies, such as the System.IO.*.

- If a project needs the functionalities of specific .NET types, use the .NET Framework until all of the functionalities your project requires are available in .NET Core and .NET BCL/FCL Core.

- The architecture for some implementations should be organized with the purpose of encapsulating and simplifying the use of resources available in .NET Core data types in BCL assemblies and namespaces, via managed and unmanaged APIs.

- When developing custom libraries for .NET Core, consider the use of internal libraries as an architectural model for distribution and organization of responsibilities.

- You should encapsulate .NET Core data types in BCL/FCL assemblies and namespaces to avoid exposing any specific kind of data type directly through your .NET Core custom libraries' programming interfaces.

- Be aware that the .NET Core runtime and the infrastructure components of .NET Core as a whole are the bases for all Microsoft .NET investments from now on. This non-specific development platform is available for Microsoft Windows, Linux distributions, and Apple macOS platforms. This opens up new opportunities for application developers, library developers, and component developers.

- Understand the general concepts, ideas, and organizational distributions that apply to the .NET Core data types that you are using in your custom libraries, such as the BCL assemblies and the namespaces of System.IO.*.

- When necessary, work with a higher-level API in your code and consider APIs that abstract the details of a more specific operating system and low-level programming.

- If you are planning to migrate a big application such as an ERP or CRM to .NET Core, remember to establish business goals for multiplatform opportunities and do not focus only on technical aspects.

- Use .NET Core 3.1 LTS to start any big migration to the .NET Core platform.

- Consider encapsulating specialized .NET Core data types via custom data types to help

  - protect the conceptual model of your custom library.

  - manage updates of .NET Core BCL System.IO.* through your custom libraries.

  - manage updates of .NET Core infrastructure throughout your custom libraries' APIs.

  - update the management of your custom libraries' APIs in future fixes, when necessary.

Don'ts

- Ignore the use of condition compilation symbols such as NETCOREAPP3_1, netstandard2_1, DEBUG, and others for the creation of more powerful source code bases.

- Encapsulate every member of every .NET Core data type in System.IO.* namespaces, or other namespaces, in a data type in a custom library "equivalent" data type.

- Create a mapping between encapsulated .NET Core data types one-by-one without a specific good technical reason or good business goal.

- Start a project using a version earlier than .NET Core 3.1 LTS.

- Consider any big migration to .NET Core until all of the functionalities that the project requires are available in .NET Core and .NET BCL/FCL Core, especially Microsoft Windows Forms and Microsoft WPF.

- Create "workarounds" for .NET type functionalities when the objectives are not the use of low-level API.

- Define goals based on superficial technical observations about .NET Core. Do create pieces of software based on the required functionalities of your applications, libraries, and components, and then make objective tests.

CHAPTER 3

Custom Data Types for a Custom Library

In this chapter, you will learn how to implement custom data types using .NET Core System.IO features and organization.

Purpose of Custom Data Types

As mentioned in a previous chapter, you should encapsulate .NET Core data types in the BCL System.IO.* namespaces to avoid exposing any specific kind of .NET Core data type in BCL System.IO.* directly through your .NET Core RVJ.IO custom library programming interfaces.

The encapsulation of custom data types of the RVJ.IO custom library should be organized around the .NET reference type and .NET value type concepts.

You saw as an example a .NET enumeration type that is a .NET value type, and you have common .NET Core enumerations that should be encapsulated in custom data types of a custom library.

The System.Enum is a .NET reference type that is an abstract class directly derived from the System.ValueType .NET reference type that implements the System.IComparable, System.IConvertible, and System. IFormattable interfaces, which are .NET reference types too.

Figure 3-1 shows an excerpt of the declaration of the System.Enum .NET Core value type, as is in the Microsoft official documentation.

© Roger Villela 2020
R. Villela, *Understanding System.IO for .NET Core 3*,
https://doi.org/10.1007/978-1-4842-5872-9_3

```C#
                                                              Copy
[System.Runtime.InteropServices.ComVisible(true)]
[System.Serializable]
public abstract class Enum : ValueType, IComparable, IConvertible,
IFormattable
```

Figure 3-1. *Declaration of the the System.Enum .NET Core value type as in the Microsoft official documentation*

In the C# programming language, the keyword *enum* is used to declare a new .NET reference type derived directly from the *abstract System.Enum* .NET reference type. In fact, by doing this you are asking the C# compiler to implement a derivation of System.Enum for you and implement all the necessary infrastructure code.

The code in Listing 3-1 and Listing 3-2 encapsulates common members of the System.IO.DriveType. Figure 3-2 shows the C# code, and Figure 3-3 shows the MSIL for this enum implementation.

Listing 3-1. Encapsulating Common Members of System. IO.DriveType

```
using System;
#if DEBUG
using System.Diagnostics;
#endif

namespace RVJ.IO {
    public enum DriveType : System.UInt32 {
        Fixed = System.IO.DriveType.Fixed,
    Ram = System.IO.DriveType.Ram,
    Network = System.IO.DriveType.Network,
    CDRom = System.IO.DriveType.CDRom,
    Removable = System.IO.DriveType.Removable
    };
};
```

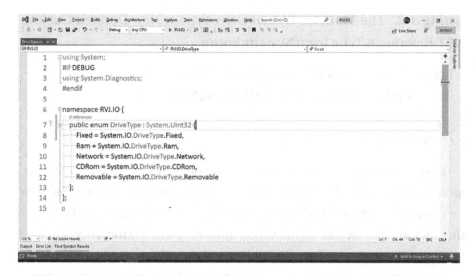

Figure 3-2. *Showing RVJ.IO examples of data types encapsulating functionalities of .NET Core data types of the BCL System.IO namespace*

Figure 3-3. *MSIL shown in the ILDASM tool of .NET Core SDK*

Listing 3-2 and Listing 3-3 show the MSIL for declaring and extending from System.Enum the new custom .NET reference type RVJ.IO.DriveType.

Listing 3-2. The MSIL for RVJ.IO.DriveType, a New Derived Custom .NET Reference Type from System.Enum

```
.class public auto ansi sealed RVJ.IO.DriveType
       extends [System.Runtime]System.Enum
{
} // end of class RVJ.IO.DriveType
```

Listing 3-3 shows some enumeration members of System.IO.DriveType encapsulated in a RVJ.IO.DriveType enumeration in MSIL. The members for the values in the enum are declared as fields with public access and static. Also, they are declared as literal values, indicating that the member is not pointing to an instance of another object and the value is used as defined.

Another interesting aspect is that the compiler automatically creates a special field named *value*, and it is the value you have assigned to the enum when using operators such as = (assign operator).

Listing 3-3. Examples of Some Members of the RVJ.IO.DriveType

```
.class public auto ansi sealed RVJ.IO.DriveType
       extends [System.Runtime]System.Enum
{

.field public static literal valuetype RVJ.IO.DriveType CDRom =
uint32(0x00000005)

.field public static literal valuetype RVJ.IO.DriveType Fixed =
uint32(0x00000003)

.field public static literal valuetype RVJ.IO.DriveType Network
= uint32(0x00000004)

.field public static literal valuetype RVJ.IO.DriveType Ram =
uint32(0x00000006)
```

```
.field public static literal valuetype RVJ.IO.DriveType
Removable = uint32(0x00000002)
```

.field public specialname rtspecialname uint32 value__

```
} // end of class RVJ.IO.DriveType
```

It is important to remember that you must include a specific .NET Core System.IO data type as part of the encapsulated custom data types for a custom library by demand, and not just doing a map one-by-one without a specific good technical reason or good business reason. Also, you do not have to encapsulate every member of any namespaces in a data type in a custom library.

You must include custom data types that help the custom library that you are developing and simplify the use of the .NET Core System. IO namespace data types encapsulated, or.NET data types of any other assemblies and namespaces, when necessary for the custom library that you are working on.

These are patterns of organization that you should follow for the implementation of any enumeration, for example.

For the sample RVJ.IO custom library, you have more custom data types for encapsulating the System.IO enums and you are following the same pattern.

Listing 3-4 shows a derived enum that encapsulates values for the members of the System.IO.FileAccess enum.

Listing 3-4. Encapsulating Members of the System.IO.FileAccess Enum

```
using System;
#if DEBUG
using System.Diagnostics;
#endif
```

```
namespace RVJ.IO {
    public enum FileAccess : System.UInt32 {
        Read = System.IO.FileAccess.Read,
        Write = System.IO.FileAccess.Write,
        ReadAndWrite = System.IO.FileAccess.ReadWrite
    };
};
```

Listing 3-5 shows the implementation of the RVJ.IO.FileMode .NET Core enumeration that encapsulates some members of the System. IO.FileMode .NET Core enumeration.

Listing 3-5. System.IO.FileMode Members Encapsulated by RVJ. IO.FileMode

```
using System;
#if DEBUG
using System.Diagnostics;
#endif

namespace RVJ.IO {

    public enum FileMode {
        New = System.IO.FileMode.CreateNew,
                    Create = System.IO.FileMode.Create,
                    OpenOrCreate = System.IO.FileMode.
                    OpenOrCreate,
                    Open = System.IO.FileMode.Open,
                    Append = System.IO.FileMode.Append,
                    Truncate = System.IO.FileMode.Truncate
    };
};
```

Viewing the MSIL for the RVJ.IO.FileAccess and for RVJ.IO.FileMode enums, the pattern followed by the C# compiler is the same for the internal structure of the derived custom .NET Core data types from System.Enum, and this is shown in Figure 3-4 and Figure 3-5.

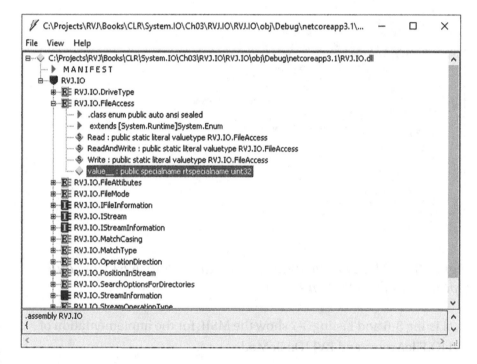

Figure 3-4. *MSIL for the RVJ.IO.FileAccess custom .NET Core data type derived from System.Enum*

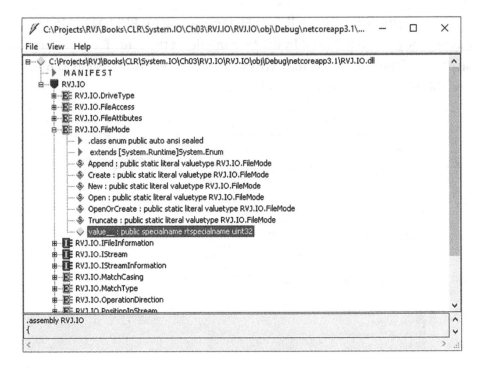

Figure 3-5. *MSIL for the RVJ.IO.FileMode custom .NET Core data type derived from System.Enum*

Listing 3-6 and Listing 3-7 show the MSIL for the implementation of RVJ.IO.FileAccess and RVJ.IO.FileMode.

Listing 3-6. MSIL for the Implementation of the RVJ.IO.FileAccess Custom Data Type Derived from System.Enum

```
.class public auto ansi sealed RVJ.IO.FileAccess
        extends [System.Runtime]System.Enum
{
.field public static literal valuetype RVJ.IO.FileAccess Read =
uint32(0x00000001)

.field public static literal valuetype RVJ.IO.FileAccess
ReadAndWrite = uint32(0x00000003)
```

```
.field public static literal valuetype RVJ.IO.FileAccess
Write = uint32(0x00000002)
```

.field public specialname rtspecialname uint32 value__

```
} // end of class RVJ.IO.FileAccess
```

Listing 3-7. MSIL for the Implementation of the RVJ.IO.FileMode
Custom Data Type Derived from System.Enum

```
.class public auto ansi sealed RVJ.IO.FileMode
       extends [System.Runtime]System.Enum
{
.field public static literal valuetype RVJ.IO.FileMode
Append = uint32(0x00000006)

.field public static literal valuetype RVJ.IO.FileMode
Create = uint32(0x00000002)

.field public static literal valuetype RVJ.IO.FileMode
New = uint32(0x00000001)

.field public static literal valuetype RVJ.IO.FileMode
Open = uint32(0x00000003)

.field public static literal valuetype RVJ.IO.FileMode
OpenOrCreate = uint32(0x00000004)

.field public static literal valuetype RVJ.IO.FileMode
Truncate = uint32(0x00000005)
```

.field public specialname rtspecialname uint32 value__

```
} // end of class RVJ.IO.FileMode
```

You can check RVJ.IO the custom library project source code and see
that there are more custom enumerations that encapsulate .NET Core
System.IO enumerations and the same model for implementation is used.

Working with Custom Data Types for Stream Data Types

When you are developing a custom library or a code base that should be used as starting point for more advanced software libraries and source code bases, you must be aware of certain details of your projects and source code.

As said before, when working with data streams, one behavior that is necessary is to get information about the data stream. But even with a platform that tries to abstract the details of the target operating system, as .NET does, you'll always need to avoid certain .NET types and their features when writing code that should be operating system agnostic.

To achieve this type of portability of source code and use of the .NET Core APIs, it is important to avoid creating .NET reference types that inherit directly or indirectly from some kind of data stream types, such as System. IO.BinaryReader or System.IO.BinaryWriter, because you will need to override complex and sometimes non-agnostic operating system source code.

It will be much more practical to use ideas and concepts for custom library actions (behaviors and events) instead of trying to replicate member-by-member something that is working and can be encapsulated.

Using the concepts and flexibility of encapsulating the useful .NET Core data types, you will be extending (not in the formal concept of OOP, but you could) and aggregating the features of the .NET Core custom data types of the specific new context of business or science, for example.

Figure 3-6 and Figure 3-7 show, for example, that the System.IO.File cannot be used as the base .NET reference type (class) because is declared with the *static* C# modifier in the class declaration.

If you are trying to use OOP as the only approach for designing a .NET Core custom data type for a custom library, you have a problem with the System.IO.File because you cannot inherit from it.

```
[System.Runtime.InteropServices.ComVisible(true)]
public static class File
```

Inheritance Object → File

Figure 3-6. *System.IO.File cannot be used as the base .NET reference type (class) because it is declared with the static C# modifier in the class declaration*

Figure 3-7. *System.IO.File cannot be used as the base .NET reference type (class)*

The System.IO.FileInfo is another important .NET reference type of System.IO data types that you will be using soon in your RVJ.IO custom library, but you cannot derive from it because the System.IO.FileInfo is declared as *sealed*.

Figure 3-8 and Figure 3-9 show a scenario similar to the System.IO.File .NET reference type, but this time because of *sealed* C# keyword that indicates that you cannot inherit from a .NET reference type declared with this keyword.

```
C#                                                            [] Copy

[System.Runtime.InteropServices.ComVisible(true)]
[System.Serializable]
public sealed class FileInfo : System.IO.FileSystemInfo
```

Figure 3-8. *System.IO.FileInfo cannot be used as the base .NET reference type (class) because is declared with the sealed C# modifier in the class declaration*

```
0 references
···public··class MyFileInfo : System.IO.FileInfo·{

                            {} namespace System
    ···}                    'MyFileInfo': cannot derive from sealed type 'FileInfo'
```

Figure 3-9. *System.IO.FileInfo cannot be used as the base .NET reference type (class)*

The .NET reference type interface is another concept that should be considered as a fundamental element in the design of custom data types. Note that .NET reference type interfaces are used in source code files IStreamInformation.cs and IStream.cs (Listing 3-8 and Listing 3-9).

The .NET Core data types in System.IO.* namespaces do the management of the input and output of operations via some type of data stream, and your RVJ.IO will encapsulate specialized behaviors of .NET Core data types available in the BCL System.IO namespace.

Listing 3-8. **Suggestion with a Sample Source Code for the .NET Core Custom Data Type IStream Public Interface**

```
using System;
#if DEBUG
using System.Diagnostics;
#endif
```

```
namespace RVJ.IO {

    public interface IStream {

        #region Behaviors
        /// <summary>
        ///  Tries to open the data stream.
        /// </summary>
        Boolean Open();
        /// <summary>
        /// Verifies if the data stream was created.
        /// </summary>
        Boolean Exists();

        /// <summary>
        /// Tries to read some portion of the data stream.
        /// Returns the read portion of data stream in  System.
        ///     Byte[] array.
        /// </summary>
        Byte[] Read( OperationDirection operationDirection,
        UInt32 numberOfBytes, Boolean asyncOperation );

        /// <summary>
        /// Tries to write to the data stream.
        /// </summary>
        Boolean Write();

        /// <summary>
        /// Tries to close the data stream.
        /// </summary>
        Boolean Close();
        #endregion

        #region Properties
```

```
        /// <summary>
        /// Base data stream object instance that was opened
            for manipulation.
        /// </summary>
        System.IO.Stream DataStream { get; set; }
        #endregion

    };

};
```

Listing 3-9. Suggestion with a Sample Source Code for the .NET
Core Custom Data Type IStreamInformation Public Interface

```
using System;
#if DEBUG
using System.Diagnostics;
#endif

namespace RVJ.IO {

public interface IStreamInformation : RVJ.IO.IStream {
#region Properties
        /// <summary>
        /// Type of data stream.
        /// </summary>
        RVJ.IO.StreamType Type { get; set; }

        /// <summary>
        /// Name of data stream (real or virtual).
        /// </summary>
        String Name { get; set; }

        /// <summary>
```

```
/// Size of data stream (32-bit). Can be zero or a
    negative value.
/// </summary>
Int32 SizeInBytes { get; set; }

/// <summary>
/// Larger size (64-bit) of a data stream, if available.
    Can be zero or a negative value.

/// </summary>
Int64 LargerSizeInBytes { get; set; }
/// <summary>
/// Date of creation of data stream.
/// </summary>
DateTime Creation { get; set; }

/// <summary>
/// Date of last update of data stream.
/// </summary>
DateTime LastUpdate { get; set; }

/// <summary>
/// Indicates the type of operation supported by the
    data stream at this moment.
/// </summary>
RVJ.IO.StreamOperationType OperatingType { get; set; }

/// <summary>
/// Indicates if an operation of read can be realized.
/// </summary>
Boolean CanRead { get; }

/// <summary>
/// Indicates if an operation of write can be realized.
```

```
        /// </summary>
        Boolean CanWrite { get; }
        #endregion

  };
};
```

Based on this concept of stream information, you can create, for example, a more specialized custom data type for getting information from a file, as shown in Listing 3-10 with the IFileInformation.cs source code file and RVJ.IO.IFileInformation that is derived from RVJ.IO.IStreamInformation.

Listing 3-10. Proposed More Specialized Custom .NET Core Data Type Interface RVJ.IO.IFileInformation Derived from RVJ. IO.IStreamInformation

```
using System;
#if DEBUG
using System.Diagnostics;
#endif

namespace RVJ.IO {
    public interface IFileInformation : RVJ.IO.IStreamInformation {

    };
};
```

For creating and implementing custom data types that are cross-platform and agnostic in terms of certain operating system functionalities, you should use more abstract ideas and concepts, based on the libraries you are using as the foundation for your custom library or libraries, such as BCL System.IO, for example.

In BCL System.IO, you can see that the concepts of enumeration, data stream, and information are three examples that you can use as the base concepts for your custom library's custom data types and behaviors.

Using C++/CLI Projection and .NET Core

When you are using .NET Core 3.1 you can use the C++/CLI projection for writing code for the .NET Core platform. The following examples show the new configurations supported by Microsoft C++ tools for developing code for the .NET Core.

You can read the following two blog posts about .NET Core 3.x and C++/CLI projection on the Microsoft official C++ Team Blog. At the time of this writing and as explained in these Microsoft official blog posts, the C++/CLI projection is available only for the Microsoft Windows operating system, for .NET Core and .NET Framework: "The Future of C++/CLI and .NET Core 3" (from September, 2019 at `https://devblogs.microsoft.com/cppblog/the-future-of-cpp-cli-and-dotnet-core-3/`) and "An Update on C++/CLI and .NET Core" (from November, 2019 at `https://devblogs.microsoft.com/cppblog/an-update-on-cpp-cli-and-dotnet-core/`).

Figure 3-10 shows the template *CLR Class Library (.NET Core)* for Microsoft Visual C++ used for the sample project, which is a .NET Core library.

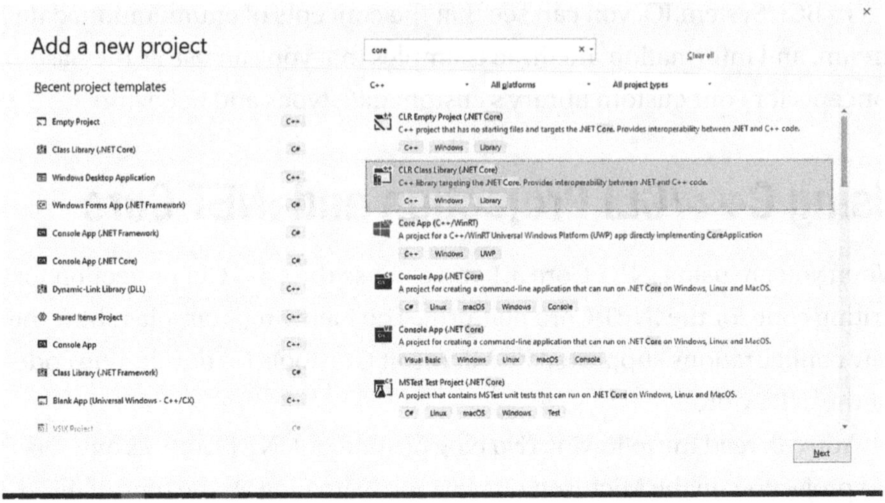

Figure 3-10. *The CLR Class Library (.NET Core) template for Microsoft Visual C++*

Figure 3-11 shows the configurations for the folders of your .NET Core Class Library written in C++/CLI projection.

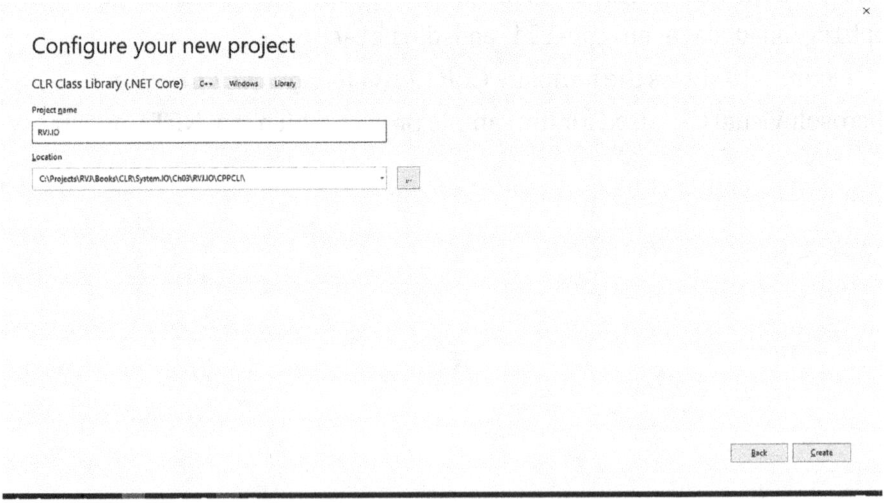

Figure 3-11. *The configurations for the folders of your .NET Core Class Library written in the C++/CLI projection*

After the project is created, open the project properties as shown in Figure 3-12 and look at the Advanced page properties.

In the C++/CLI Properties section is the Common Language Runtime Support property, as shown in Figure 3-12. This property has the compilation option */clr* with the value *netcore*, which is new for the Microsoft C++/CLI projection.

In the Advanced page property shown in Figure 3-12, you can see the property *.NET Core Target Framework* which you must set as *netcoreapp3.1* for the minimum value of your project.

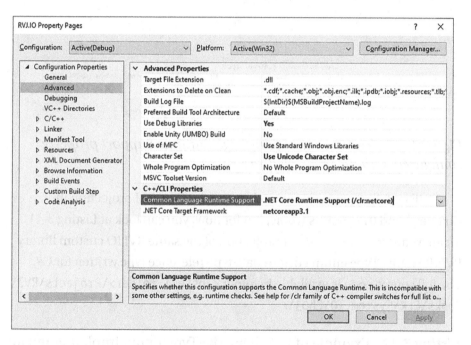

Figure 3-12.   *Project properties on the Advanced properties page*

Figure 3-13 shows another properties page, *C/C++*, where you have the *Common Language Runtime Support* property configured with the value *NetCore*, which is also a new value supported for the C++/CLI projection by the Microsoft C++ compiler option */clr*.

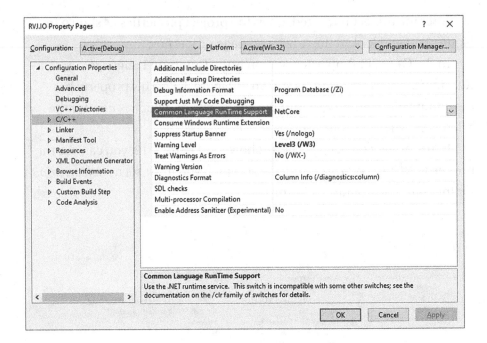

Figure 3-13. *The Common Language Runtime Support property configured with the value NetCore*

I will be talking more about code using the C++/CLI projection in Chapter 4 and the book as whole, but for now, you can look at Listing 3-11 for an example in the C++/CLI projection of the same RVJ.IO custom library RVJ::IO::DriveType enum custom data type reference type written for C#. The full source code is available in folder <install_folder>\Projects\RVJ\ Books\CLR\System.IO\Ch03\.

Listing 3-11. Example of RVJ::IO::DriveType Enum Implemented in C++/CLI Projection for the .NET Core Platform

```
#pragma once

#pragma region Header files
#pragma endregion
```

```
#pragma region Assembly Namespaces
using namespace System;
using namespace System::IO;
#pragma endregion

namespace RVJ::IO {
        public enum class DriveType : UInt32 {
                Fixed = ( UInt32 ) System::IO::DriveType::Fixed,
                Ram = ( UInt32 ) System::IO::DriveType::Ram,
                Network = ( UInt32 ) System::IO::DriveType::
                Network,
                CDRom = ( UInt32 ) System::IO::DriveType::CDRom,
                Removable = ( UInt32 ) System::IO::DriveType::
                Removable
        };
};
```

Summary

The next two sections cover recommendations about the uses of characteristics of .NET Core.

Dos

- You should encapsulate .NET Core data types in the BCL System.IO.* namespaces to avoid exposing any specific kind of .NET Core data type in BCL System.IO.* directly through your .NET Core RVJ.IO custom library programming interfaces.

- Always check the Microsoft official documentation website at `https://docs.microsoft.com/en-us/dotnet/` to learn about the model used for the organization of the .NET type.

- Always check the Microsoft official documentation to learn about the behaviors of the .NET type that the custom library is encapsulating.

- Avoid complex hierarchy of object models. Use interfaces as the starting point for abstracting the concepts and ideas.

- Identify the common concepts and organize the custom data types around them.

Don'ts

- Ignore the Microsoft official documentation as the source for learning about the concepts and functionalities available for the .NET types.

- Try to create a complex object model hierarchy just because is technically possible.

- Use a lot of abstract concepts. Instead, learn with the target contexts, such as Input/Output/Network, and create a few groups of concepts and then expand gradually using the demanded custom data types as one of the reasons for the expansions.

CHAPTER 4

Custom Collections for a Custom Library

In this chapter, you will learn the fundamental aspects of implementing custom collections using features and the organization required for any .NET platform library implementations.

Overview

When you work with collections, you follow patterns and standards, such as the behaviors you use to iterate through the instances of data types stored in an instance of a collection data type, non-generic–based or generic-based collection data type.

Any .NET library implementation that is using collections is implementing patterns and following standards, which includes the required details for the .NET platform itself.

For example, every collection in .NET libraries has a common set of base types that are required to be implemented and be used as a basis, such as the .NET interface type System.Collections.ICollection non-generic base and .NET interface type System.Collections.Generic. ICollection<T> generic base.

In this chapter, I will use the .NET class type System.Collections. ArrayList non-generic base to explain the required .NET interface types for

© Roger Villela 2020
R. Villela, *Understanding System.IO for .NET Core 3*,
https://doi.org/10.1007/978-1-4842-5872-9_4

non-generic–based collections and the .NET class type System.Collections. Generic.List<T> generic base to explain the required .NET interface types for generic-based collections.

These explanations and concepts are valid for any collection following the .NET standards for the implementation of .NET libraries. These explanations are also valid for .NET Core and .NET Framework implementations and the respective libraries, BCL or FCL, or any others for .NET implementations.

The next chapters will require this kind of knowledge because I will be talking about a custom collection for the System.IO data types, and all of the collections follow these standards of the .NET platform implementations.

Fundamental Set of .NET Data Types for Collections in BCL

As mentioned in previous chapters, you should encapsulate .NET Core data types in BCL System.IO.* namespaces to avoid exposing any specific kind of .NET Core data type in BCL System.IO.* directly through your .NET Core RVJ.IO custom library programming interfaces.

Non-Generic–Based Custom Collections

In the .NET Core BCL and .NET Framework BCL there are two base data types that should be implemented and supported, directly or indirectly, by any collection data type for the .NET platform implementations.

For all .NET non-generic–based collections, shown in Figure 4-1, we have the .NET interface type System.Collections.ICollection as the base data type, and it is available in the assemblies System.Runtime.dll, mscorlib.dll, and netstandard.dll.

Figure 4-1. *The .NET interface type System.Collections.ICollection non-generic base is the base of all .NET non-generic–based collections*

This means that the .NET interface type System.Collections.ICollection non-generic base is the base for all .NET non-generic–based data types available in the System.Collections namespace (and any others) that implement the concepts and functionalities of .NET non-generic–based collections.

In general, when you are creating a custom set of collections with a commercial purpose, a better starting pointing derives (creates a specialization) from a .NET class type collection, such as System. Collections.ArrayList non-generic base or System.Collections.Generic. List<T> generic base, for example.

However, if you are considering implementing a custom collection from the ground up, you must base your custom collections on a set of .NET interface types that are required to work with .NET environments. For example, when working with the for...each pattern in .NET compatible programming languages, the compiler infrastructure is expecting that your custom collection has implemented the required .NET interface types for collections.

81

The .NET interface type System.Collections.ICollection is one of those base collections types that are required.

Talking specifically about the .NET interface type System.Collections. ICollection as an example, you should be aware that the following members and respective behaviors are required to be implemented:

- Properties

  - Count

    - `https://docs.microsoft.com/en-us/dotnet/ api/system.collections.icollection. count?view=netcore-3.1#System_ Collections_ICollection_Count`

    - `https://docs.microsoft.com/en-us/dotnet/ api/system.collections.icollection. count?view=netframework-4.8#System_ Collections_ICollection_Count`

  - IsSynchronized

    - `https://docs.microsoft.com/en-us/dotnet/ api/system.collections.icollection. issynchronized?view=netcore-3.1#System_ Collections_ICollection_IsSynchronized`

    - `https://docs.microsoft.com/en-us/dotnet/ api/system.collections.icollection.issyn chronized?view=netframework-4.8`

  - SyncRoot

    - `https://docs.microsoft.com/en-us/dotnet/ api/system.collections.icollection. syncroot?view=netcore-3.1#System_ Collections_ICollection_SyncRoot`

- https://docs.microsoft.com/en-us/dotnet/
  api/system.collections.icollection.
  syncroot?view=netframework-4.8

- Methods

  - CopyTo()

    - https://docs.microsoft.com/en-us/dotnet/
      api/system.collections.icollection.
      copyto?view=netcore-3.1#System_
      Collections_ICollection_CopyTo_System_
      Array_System_Int32_

    - https://docs.microsoft.com/en-us/dotnet/
      api/system.collections.icollection.
      copyto?view=netframework-4.8

  - **System.Collections.IEnumerable.
    GetEnumerator() (inherited from System.
    Collections.IEnumerable)**

    - https://docs.microsoft.com/en-us/dotnet/
      api/system.collections.ienumerable.
      getenumerator?view=netcore-3.1#System_
      Collections_IEnumerable_GetEnumerator

    - https://docs.microsoft.com/en-us/dotnet/
      api/system.collections.ienumerable.geten
      umerator?view=netframework-4.8

Reading about these members, in particular about the methods, will give you information about the method with GetEnumerator() as the name; it is part of another .NET interface type, the System.Collections. IEnumerable.

The point here is a common aspect for the .NET types: a set of .NET interface types are related based on inheritance between contracts. That is, instead of a .NET class type declared with multiple .NET interface types at the class level, the .NET class type is declared with few .NET interface types, but they are composed of a succession of .NET interface types that, in the final, creates the full expected collection type with the required behaviors and concepts available.

Figure 4-2 shows the .NET collections available in the System. Collections namespace (or in any others) using the **.NET API Browser** tool for .NET Core libraries and .NET Framework libraries (see `https://docs.microsoft.com/en-us/dotnet/api/?view=netcore-3.1`).

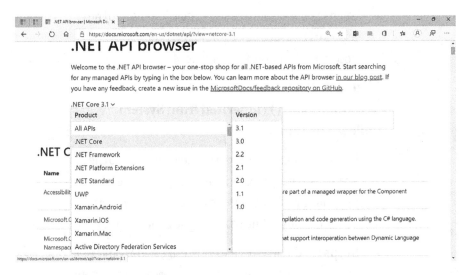

Figure 4-2. *Using the .NET API Browser tool to inspect all the .NET APIs available for and based on .NET Core libraries*

For example, the .NET class type System.Collections.ArrayList non-generic–base is a collection that implements the .NET interface type System.Collections.ICollection inherited through the .NET interface type System.Collections.IList non-generic–base, which extends the .NET interface type System.Collections.ICollection.

Listing 4-1 and Figure 4-3 are based on Microsoft official documentation and show the C# code with a declaration of the .NET interface type System.Collections.IList non-generic base.

Listing 4-1. C# Code with the Declaration of the System.Collections. IList That Extends the System.Collections.ICollection

```
[System.Runtime.InteropServices.ComVisible(true)]
public interface IList : System.Collections.ICollection
```

```
C#

[System.Runtime.InteropServices.ComVisible(true)]
public interface IList : System.Collections.ICollection
```

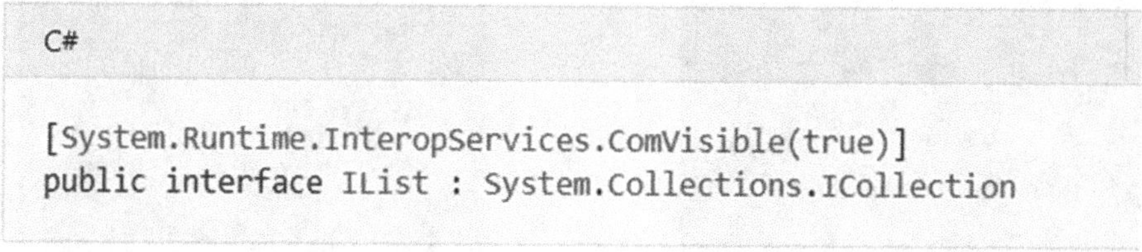

Figure 4-3. *The .NET interface type System.Collections.IList extends the .NET interface type System.Collections.ICollection, and both are implemented by the .NET class type System.Collections.ArrayList non-generic–based collection*

Figure 4-4 shows the sequence with a composition to help you understand the relationship between the .NET class type System. Collections.ArrayList, used as an example, and the .NET interface types that it is based on.

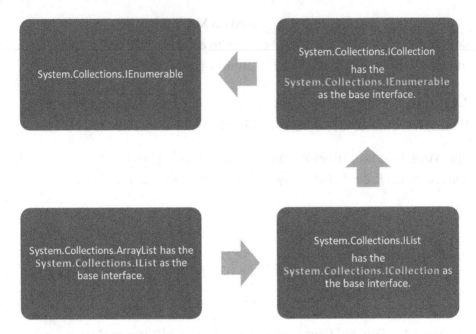

Figure 4-4. *System.Collections.ArrayList implements the .NET interface types System.Collections.IList, System.Collections. ICollection, and System.Collections.IEnumerable*

Generic-Based Custom Collections

All collections that are based on .NET generic technology have the .NET interface type System.Collections.Generic.ICollection<T> generic base as the base type (see Figure 4-5), and it is available in the assemblies System. Runtime.dll, mscorlib.dll, and netstandard.dll.

Figure 4-5. *The .NET interface type System.Collections.Generic. ICollection<T> generic base is the base of all .NET generic-based collections*

This means that the .NET interface type System.Collections.Generic. ICollection<T> generic base is the base interface for all .NET generic-based data types available in the System.Collections.Generic namespace that implement the concepts and functionalities of .NET generic-based collections.

For example, the .NET class type System.Collections.Generic.List<T> generic base is a collection that implements the .NET interface type System.Collections.Generic.ICollection<T> through the .NET interface type System.Collections.Generic.IList<T> generic base that extends the .NET interface type System.Collections.Generic.ICollection<T>.

Figure 4-6, based on Microsoft official documentation, shows the declaration of .NET class type System.Collections.Generic.List<T> with the fundamental .NET interface types that are implemented by the .NET class type.

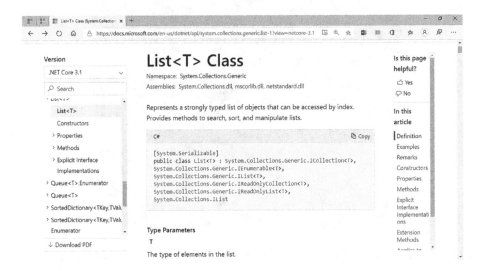

Figure 4-6. *.NET class type System.Collections.Generic.List<T> declaration with the fundamental set of .NET interface types shown*

In the Microsoft official documentation, the text explicitly shows the .NET interface types on which the .NET class type System.Collections. Generic.List<T> is based. The purpose is to help the readers of the documentation to quickly find the relationship between the .NET class type and the fundamental set of base .NET interface types implemented by the .NET class type .NET System.Collections.Generic.List<T>, in this case.

Figure 4-7 shows an excerpt of Microsoft official source code for the .NET Framework Class Library 4.8 .NET class type System.Collections. Generic.List<T> implementation.

Figure 4-7.   *.NET class type System.Collections.Generic.List<T>
is declared as implementing System.Collections.Generic.IList<T>,
System.Collections.IList, and System.Collections.Generic.
IReadOnlyList<T>. (Microsoft Official Reference Source)*

Figure 4-8 shows an excerpt of the Microsoft official **.NET Core
Source Browser** tool source code repository for the .NET Core Base
Class Library 3.1 .NET class type System.Collections.Generic.List<T>
implementation.

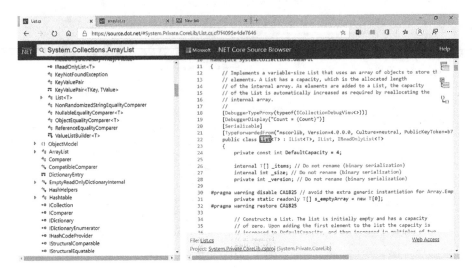

Figure 4-8. *.NET class type System.Collections.Generic.List<T>
is declared as implementing System.Collections.Generic.IList<T>,
System.Collections.IList, and System.Collections.Generic.
IReadOnlyList<T>. (Microsoft Official .NET Core Source Browser)*

For the set of .NET interface types shown on the page of the Microsoft
official documentation, the following quick explanations are helpful:

- The .NET interface type System.Collections.Generic.
  IList<T> generic base is the base interface for some of the
  behaviors that characterize the implementation of a list
  as a dynamic, resizable container-based collection and
  has the .NET interface type System.Collections.Generic.
  ICollection<T> generic base as the base .NET interface type.

- The .NET interface type System.Collections.Generic.
  ICollection<T> generic base is shown because it is
  the base .NET interface type for all collections for the
  .NET platform libraries. As mentioned, if you want to
  implement a custom .NET collection, it's important to
  learn about these foundational data types for the model
  used by .NET platform for the libraries.

- The .NET interface type System.Collections.Generic.
  IEnumerable<T> generic base is shown because it
  is required by collections with the support for the
  behaviors required for iteration over the instances of
  data types stored in the instance of a collection. Also,
  because the .NET interface type System.Collections.
  Generic.ICollection<T> has as the base type the
  .NET interface type System.Collections.Generic.
  IEnumerable<T>.

- You can have a read-only collection or a read/write
  collection, and the .NET interface type System.
  Collections.Generic.IReadOnlyList<T> aggregates the
  required concepts and behaviors of the read-only to
  a read/write collection type. The .NET interface type
  System.Collections.Generic.IReadOnlyList<T> generic
  base has as the base the .NET interface type System.
  Collections.Generic.IReadOnlyCollection<T>, that
  has as the base the .NET interface type the System.
  Collections.Generic.IEnumerable<T> generic base.

Listing 4-2 and Figure 4-9, based on Microsoft official documentation,
show the C# code with a declaration for the .NET interface type System.
Collections.Generic.IList<T> generic base.

Listing 4-2. C# Code with the Declaration of the .NET Interface
Type System.Collections.Generic.IList<T> That Extends the .NET
Interface Type System.Collections.Generic.ICollection<T>

```
public interface IList<T> :
System.Collections.Generic.ICollection<T>,
System.Collections.Generic.IEnumerable<T>
```

```
C#

public interface IList<T> :
System.Collections.Generic.ICollection<T>,
System.Collections.Generic.IEnumerable<T>
```

Figure 4-9. *The .NET interface type System.Collections.Generic. IList<T> extends the .NET interface type System.Collections.Generic. ICollection<T>, and both are implemented by the .NET class type System.Collections.Generic.List<T> generic-based collection*

As the scenario I described for the Microsoft official documentation for the .NET class type System.Collections.Generic.List<T> and the set of .NET interface types shown, in the Microsoft official documentation for the .NET interface type System.Collections.Generic.IList<T>, and as shown in Figure 4-10 in the remarks section of the Microsoft official documentation, there is some information about the relationship of the two .NET interface types and the role of the System.Collections.Generic.ICollection<T> as the base .NET interface type for all .NET generic-based collections for the .NET platform implementations.

Remarks

The IList<T> generic interface is a descendant of the ICollection<T> generic interface and is the base interface of all generic lists.

Figure 4-10. *The .NET interface type System.Collections.Generic. IList<T> is based on the System.Collections.Generic.ICollection<T> that has the .NET interface type System.Collections.Generic. IEnumerable<T> as the base interface type*

Figure 4-11 shows an excerpt of C# code for .NET interface type System.Collections.Generic.IList<T> from the Microsoft .NET Core Source Browser tool at https://source.dot.net.

Figure 4-11. *Excerpt of C# code of .NET interface type System. Collections.Generic.IList<T> (Microsoft Official .NET Core Source browser)*

Figure 4-12 shows an excerpt of the C# code for the .NET interface type System.Collections.Generic.IList<T> from the Microsoft Reference Source page at `https://referencesource.microsoft.com/`.

Figure 4-12. *.NET interface type System.Collections.Generic.IList<T> is the **base interface for all generic lists** and inherits from System. Collections.Generic.ICollection<T> .NET interface type. (Microsoft Official Reference Source)*

Iteration Over Collections

As shown in Figure 4-13, when working with collections, you follow patterns, such as the behaviors that you use to iterate through the instances of data types stored in an instance of a collection data type, non-generic–based or generic-based.

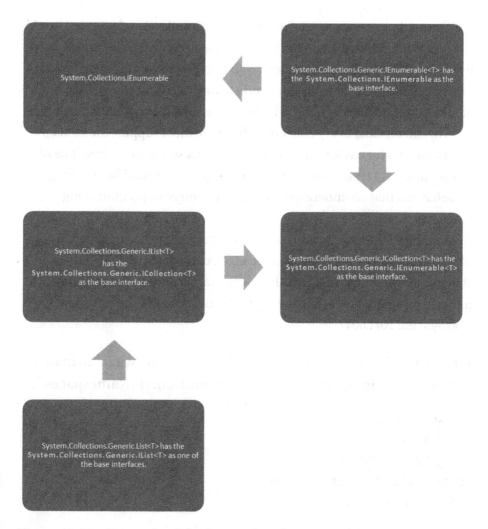

Figure 4-13. *Example of the hierarchy of .NET interface types implemented by the .NET class type System.Collections.Generic. List<T> generic base*

When you use the for...each pattern via the respective syntaxes in any programming language or environment, you do so because various concepts and patterns of collections are supported on these respective technological contexts.

One of these concepts that an instance of a collection data type should support is the capacity to be iterated or to be navigated. For example, when using the for...each pattern, you implement by the collection data type the behaviors that allow your code to navigate between instances of elements (referenced by) stored in the instance of that collection data type.

This means that every collection data type must support the concepts and behaviors for navigation between elements stored in the instance of a collection data type. This iteration, or navigation, should be provided by behaviors that are independent of the statement or programming language.

Listing 4-3 shows that you can iterate over a sequence of instances of data types stored in an instance of a collection data type using the statements for each, for, and while, for example. Open the solution/ project Lesson01/Iteration_over_a_collection at <install_folder>/ CLR/System.IO/Ch04/.

Listing 4-3. Iteration Over a Collection Data Type Available in the System.Collections and System.Collections.Generic Namespaces

```
#region Namespaces
using System;
using System.Collections;
using System.Collections.Generic;
#endregion

namespace Lesson01 {
    public class Program {

        static void Main() {

            String[] values = { "0", "1", "2", "3", "4", "5",
                                "6", "7", "8", "9" };
            UInt32[] numbers = { 0, 1, 2, 3, 4, 5, 6, 7, 8, 9 };
```

```
#region List of numbers using a non-generic based
collection.
ArrayList nonGenericsList = new ArrayList();
nonGenericsList.AddRange( values );
#endregion

#region List of numbers using a generic based
collection.
List<UInt32> genericsList = new List<UInt32>();
genericsList.AddRange( numbers );
#endregion

foreach ( String number in nonGenericsList )
Console.WriteLine( "{0}\n", number );

IEnumerator enumerator = nonGenericsList.
GetEnumerator();
while ( enumerator.MoveNext() ) Console.WriteLine(
"{0}\n", enumerator.Current.ToString() );

foreach ( UInt32 number in genericsList ) Console.
WriteLine( "{0}\n", number.ToString() );

IEnumerator<UInt32> enumeratorGenerics =
genericsList.GetEnumerator();
while ( enumeratorGenerics.MoveNext() ) Console.
WriteLine( "{0}\n", enumeratorGenerics.Current.
ToString() );

UInt32 index = new UInt32();
UInt32 length = ( ( UInt32 ) nonGenericsList.Count );

for ( String[] items = ( String[] )
nonGenericsList.ToArray(); index < length; index++
) Console.WriteLine( "{0}\n", items[ index
].ToString() );
```

```
        length = ( ( UInt32 ) genericsList.Count );
        index = new UInt32();

        for ( UInt32[] items = genericsList.ToArray();
        index < length; index++ ) Console.WriteLine
        ( "{0}\n", items[ index ].ToString() );


    }
  };
};
```

Figure 4-14 shows the signature for one of the constructors of the .NET class type System.Collections.ArrayList non-generic–based collection.

C#

```
public ArrayList (System.Collections.ICollection c);
```

Parameters

c   ICollection

The ICollection whose elements are copied to the new list.

Figure 4-14. *Signature of the constructor that requires an argument value with the base .NET interface type System.Collections.ICollection implemented*

The signature of this constructor indicates that the argument value is required to be based on an implementation of the .NET interface type System.Collections.ICollection; this means an instance of a .NET class type that has this .NET interface type implemented, directly or indirectly.

This kind of information about .NET data type relationships is also used by tools, as shown in Figure 4-15, and the sample code with the IntelliSense of Microsoft Visual Studio/Visual C# shows the signature of the constructor with System.Collections.ICollection as the parameter data type.

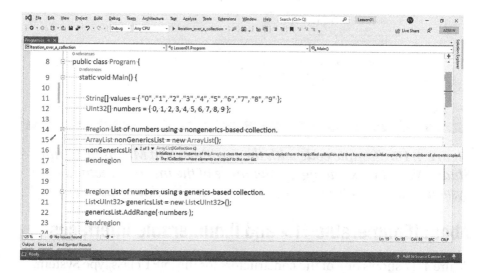

Figure 4-15. *Sample code with the IntelliSense of Microsoft Visual Studio/Visual C# showing the signature of the constructor with System.Collections.ICollection as the parameter data type*

Not just the constructor of a .NET type can define a parameter of .NET interface type System.Collections.ICollection. Figure 4-16 shows the System.Collections.ArrayList.AddRange() instance method defined with a parameter of the .NET interface type System.Collections.ICollection.

```
8    public class Program {
          0 references
9        static void Main() {
10
11           String[] values = { "0", "1", "2", "3", "4", "5", "6", "7", "8", "9" };
12           UInt32[] numbers = { 0, 1, 2, 3, 4, 5, 6, 7, 8, 9 };
13
14           #region List of numbers using a nongenerics-based collection.
15           ArrayList nonGenericsList = new ArrayList();
16           nonGenericsList.AddRange( values );
17               void ArrayList.AddRange(ICollection c)
18               Adds the elements of an ICollection to the end of the ArrayList.
                 c: The ICollection whose elements should be added to the end of the ArrayList. The collection itself cannot be null, but it can contain elements that are null.
19
20           #region List of numbers using a generics-based collection.
21           List<UInt32> genericsList = new List<UInt32>();
22           genericsList.AddRange( numbers );
23           #endregion
```

Figure 4-16. *Sample code with the IntelliSense of Microsoft Visual Studio/Visual C# showing the signature of the instance method with System.Collections.ICollection as the parameter data type*

About IEnumerable<T> and IEnumerable Interfaces

Figure 4-17 shows one of the constructors for the .NET class type System. Collections.Generic.List<T> generic-based collection and indicates the argument value is required to be based on the implementation of the .NET interface type System.Collections.Generic.IEnumerable<T>, or inherited from a .NET class type that has this .NET interface type implemented, directly or indirectly.

```
C#

public List (System.Collections.Generic.IEnumerable<T>
collection);
```

Parameters

collection   IEnumerable<T>

The collection whose elements are copied to the new list.

Figure 4-17. Signature of the constructor that requires an argument value with the base .NET interface type System.Collections.Generic. IEnumerable<T> implemented

The signature of the constructor indicates that the argument value is required to be based on an implementation of the .NET interface type System.Collections.Generic.IEnumerable<T> generic base; this means an instance of a .NET class type that has this .NET interface type implemented, directly or indirectly.

This kind of information about .NET data type relationships is also used by tools, as shown in Figure 4-18 by the sample code with the IntelliSense of Microsoft Visual Studio/Visual C# showing the signature of the constructor with System.Collections.Generic.IEnumerable<T> as the parameter data type.

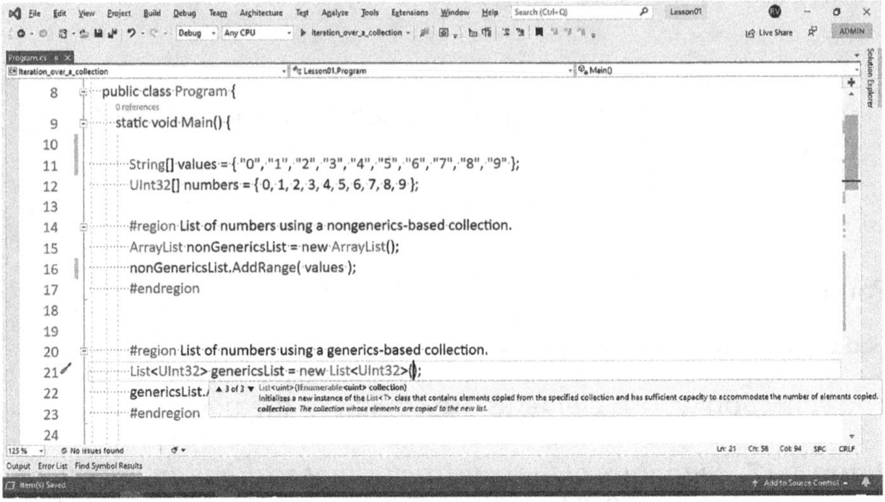

Figure 4-18. *Sample code with the IntelliSense of Microsoft Visual Studio/Visual C# showing the signature of the constructor with System.Collections.Generic.IEnumerable as the parameter data type*

Figure 4-19 shows the signature of the System.Collections.Generic. List<T>.AddRange() instance method with a defined parameter with the .NET interface type System.Collections.Generic.IEnumerable<T>.

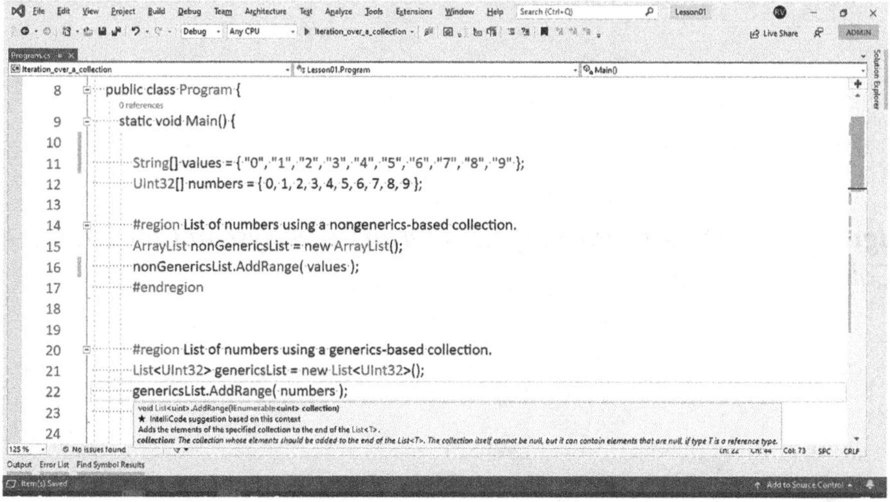

Figure 4-19. *Sample code with the IntelliSense of Microsoft Visual Studio/Visual C# showing the signature of the instance method with System.Collections.Generic.IEnumerable<T> as the parameter data type*

Listing 4-4, Listing 4-5, Figure 4-20, and Figure 4-21 (based on the Microsoft official documentation) show the declarations of the .NET interface type System.Collections.ICollection non-generic base and .NET interface type System.Collections.Generic.ICollection<T> generic base.

Listing 4-4. Source Code in C# Showing the Declaration of the .NET Interface Type System.Collections.ICollection Non-Generic Base

```
public interface ICollection : System.Collections.IEnumerable
```

Listing 4-5. Source Code in C# Showing the Declaration of the .NET Interface Type System.Collections.Generic.ICollection<T> Generic Base

```
public interface ICollection<T> : System.Collections.Generic.
IEnumerable<T>
```

```
C#

[System.Runtime.InteropServices.ComVisible(true)]
public interface ICollection : System.Collections.IEnumerable
```

Figure 4-20. *Declaration of .NET interface type System.Collections. ICollection non-generic base*

```
C#

public interface ICollection<T> :
System.Collections.Generic.IEnumerable<T>
```

Figure 4-21. *Declaration of .NET interface type System.Collections. Generic.ICollection<T> generic base*

The .NET interface type System.Collections.ICollection non-generic base extends the .NET interface type System.Collections.IEnumerable non-generic base, as shown in Figure 4-22.

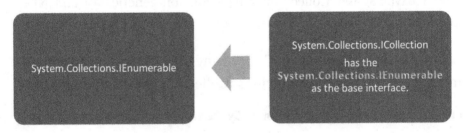

Figure 4-22. *The interface type System.Collections.ICollection .NET non-generic base extends the interface type System.Collections. IEnumerable .NET non-generic base*

The .NET interface type System.Collections.IEnumerable non-generic base provides the behaviors that every collection should implement to have the characteristics required for iteration over the instances of data types stored in an instance of a collection, using the for...each pattern or not.

As shown in Figure 4-23, the .NET interface type System.Collections. Generic.ICollection<T> generic base extends the .NET interface type System.Collections.Generic.IEnumerable<T> generic base, which extends the .NET interface type System.Collections.IEnumerable non-generic base. This means that all collections that are .NET generic-based data types should implement the members of all these .NET interface type contracts.

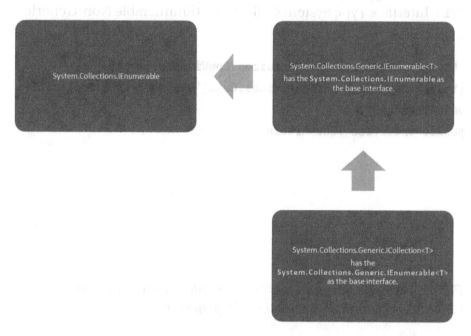

Figure 4-23. *The .NET interface type System.Collections.Generic. ICollection<T> generic base extends the .NET interface type System. Collections.Generic.IEnumerable<T> generic base, which extends the .NET interface type System.Collections.IEnumerable non-generic base*

Listing 4-6, Listing 4-7, Figure 4-24, and Figure 4-25 (based on the Microsoft official documentation) show the declarations of both .NET interface types System.Collections.IEnumerable and System.Collections. Generic.IEnumerable<T>.

Listing 4-6. Source Code in C# Showing the Declaration for the
.NET Interface Type System.Collections.Generic.IEnumerable<T>
Generic Base

```
public interface IEnumerable<out T> : System.Collections.
IEnumerable
```

Listing 4-7. Source Code in C# Showing the Declaration for the
.NET Interface Type System.Collections.IEnumerable Non-Generic
Base

```
[System.Runtime.InteropServices.ComVisible(true)]
[System.Runtime.InteropServices.Guid("496B0ABE-CDEE-11d3-88E8-
00902754C43A")]
public interface IEnumerable
```

```
C#

public interface IEnumerable<out T> :
System.Collections.IEnumerable
```

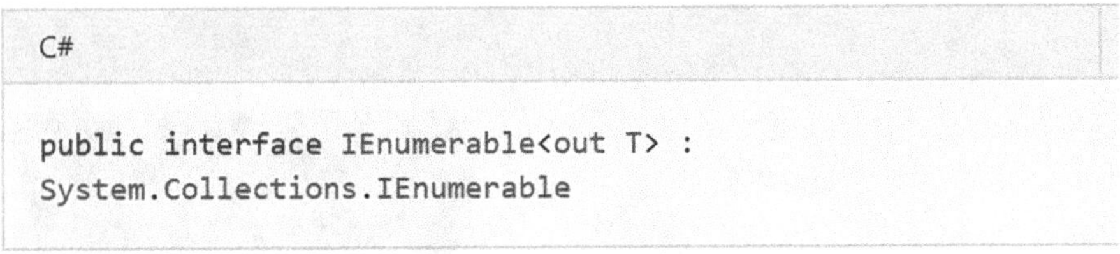

Figure 4-24. *Declaration for the .NET interface type System.
Collections.Generic.IEnumerable<T> generic base*

```
C#

[System.Runtime.InteropServices.ComVisible(true)]
[System.Runtime.InteropServices.Guid("496B0ABE-CDEE-11d3-88E8-
00902754C43A")]
public interface IEnumerable
```

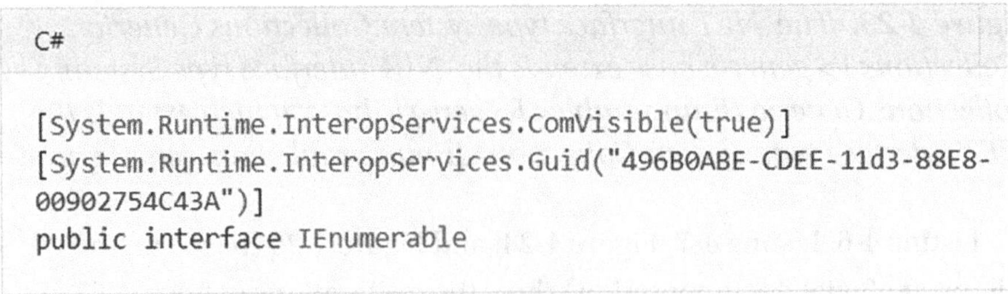

Figure 4-25. *Declaration for the .NET interface type System.
Collections.IEnumerable non-generic base*

The .NET interface type System.Collections.Generic.IEnumerable<T> generic base has as its base interface type the .NET interface type System. Collections.IEnumerable non-generic base.

Iteration Over a Collection, the Enumerator Pattern

The "simple" iteration over the instances of data types that are the elements stored in an instance of a collection is provided by a pattern called iterator or enumerator.

The *enumerator* is another concept and pattern used with collections; it's exposed through these interface types such as the .NET interface type System.Collections.IEnumerable non-generic base and .NET interface type System.Collections.Generic.IEnumerable<T> generic base.

For the enumerator pattern, the .NET interface type System. Collections.IEnumerator is the base type for all .NET non-generic–based enumerators and the .NET interface type System.Collections.Generic. IEnumerator<T> is the base type for all .NET generic-based enumerators.

Listing 4-8, Listing 4-9, Figure 4-26, and Figure 4-27 (based on the Microsoft official documentation) show the C# code with declarations for the .NET interface type System.Collections.IEnumerator non-generic base and .NET interface type System.Collections.Generic.IEnumerator<T> generic base.

Listing 4-8. C# Code with the Declaration of the .NET Interface Type System.Collections.IEnumerator Non-Generic Base

```
[System.Runtime.InteropServices.ComVisible(true)] [System.
Runtime.InteropServices.Guid("496B0ABF-CDEE-11d3-88E8-
00902754C43A")] public interface IEnumerator
```

Listing 4-9. C# Code with the Declaration of .NET Interface Type System.Collections.Generic.IEnumerator<T> Generic Base

```
public interface IEnumerator<out T> : IDisposable, System.
Collections.IEnumerator
```

```
C#

[System.Runtime.InteropServices.ComVisible(true)]
[System.Runtime.InteropServices.Guid("496B0ABF-CDEE-11d3-88E8-
00902754C43A")]
public interface IEnumerator
```

Figure 4-26. *Declaration of .NET interface type System.Collections. IEnumerator non-generic base*

```
C#

public interface IEnumerator<out T> : IDisposable,
System.Collections.IEnumerator
```

Figure 4-27. *Declaration of .NET interface type System.Collections. Generic.IEnumerator<T> generic base*

The .NET interface type System.Collections.IEnumerator non-generic base has the following members:

- Properties
  - Current
    - https://docs.microsoft.com/en-us/dotnet/ api/system.collections.ienumerator. current?view=netcore-3.1#System_ Collections_IEnumerator_Current

- https://docs.microsoft.com/en-us/dotnet/
  api/system.collections.ienumerator.
  current?view=netframework-4.8#System_
  Collections_IEnumerator_Current

- Methods

  - MoveNext()

    - https://docs.microsoft.com/en-us/dotnet/
      api/system.collections.ienumerator.
      movenext?view=netcore-3.1#System_
      Collections_IEnumerator_MoveNext

    - https://docs.microsoft.com/en-us/dotnet/
      api/system.collections.ienumerator.
      movenext?view=netframework-4.8#System_
      Collections_IEnumerator_MoveNext

  - Reset()

    - https://docs.microsoft.com/en-us/dotnet/
      api/system.collections.ienumerator.
      reset?view=netcore-3.1#System_
      Collections_IEnumerator_Reset

    - https://docs.microsoft.com/en-us/dotnet/
      api/system.collections.ienumerator.
      reset?view=netframework-4.8#System_
      Collections_IEnumerator_Reset

Figure 4-28, Figure 4-29, and Figure 4-30 show the .NET class type implementation of the System.Collections.ArrayList instance method that is the implementation for the .NET interface type System.Collections. IEnumerable.GetEnumerator() instance method.

Figure 4-28. *The .NET interface type implementation of the System. Collections.IEnumerable.GetEnumerator() instance method in .NET class type System.Collections.ArrayList (Microsoft official Reference Source repository)*

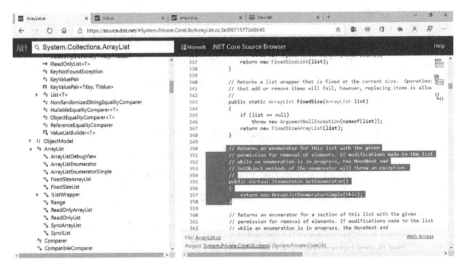

Figure 4-29. *The .NET interface type implementation of the System. Collections.IEnumerable.GetEnumerator() instance method in .NET class type System.Collections.ArrayList (Microsoft official .NET Core Source Browser repository)*

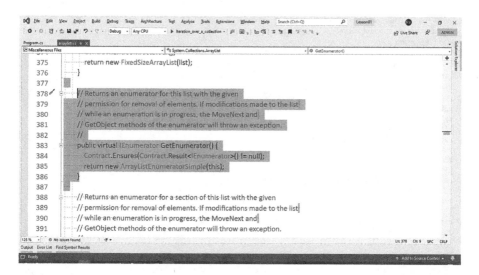

Figure 4-30. *The .NET interface type implementation of the System. Collections.IEnumerable.GetEnumerator() instance method in .NET class type System.Collections.ArrayList. (Microsoft Source Code of ArrayList.cs shown in the Microsoft Visual Studio/Visual C# source code editor)*

This .NET class type System.Collections.ArrayList.GetEnumerator instance method returns an instance of a .NET class type System. Collections.ArrayList.ArrayListEnumeratorSimple that is private and sealed; that is, it cannot be viewed or accessed from outside the scope of the declaring type, and no other .NET class type can inherit from it.

The .NET interface type System.Collections.IEnumerator is implemented by the .NET class type System.Collections.ArrayList. ArrayListEnumeratorSimple.

Figure 4-31 shows an excerpt of C# code for the implementation of the .NET class type System.Collections.ArrayList.ArrayListEnumeratorSimple.

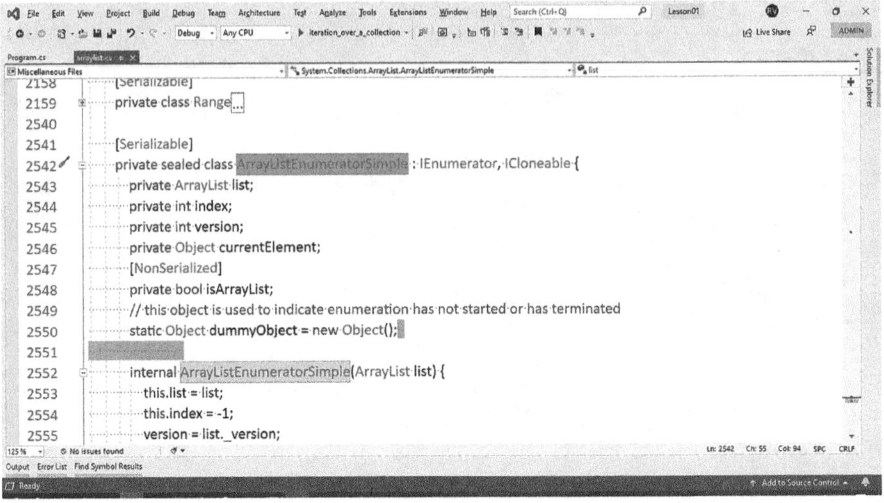

Figure 4-31. *The .NET class type System.Collections.ArrayList. ArrayListEnumeratorSimple implements the .NET interface type System.Collections.IEnumerator*

Listing 4-10 shows the use of these members of the .NET interface type System.Collections.IEnumerator.

Listing 4-10. An Enumerator Is Required by .NET Implementations and Certain Features for Collections

```
String[] values = { "0", "1", "2", "3", "4", "5", "6", "7",
"8", "9" };

#region List of string values using a non-generic based collection.
ArrayList nonGenericsList = new ArrayList();
nonGenericsList.AddRange( values );
#endregion

foreach ( String value in nonGenericsList ) Console.WriteLine
( "{0}\n", value );
```

```
IEnumerator enumerator = nonGenericsList.GetEnumerator();
while ( enumerator.MoveNext() ) Console.WriteLine( "{0}\n",
enumerator.Current.ToString() );

UInt32 index = new UInt32();
UInt32 length = ( ( UInt32 ) nonGenericsList.Count );

for ( String[] items = ( String[] ) nonGenericsList.ToArray();
index < length; index++ ) Console.WriteLine( "{0}\n", items[
index ] );
```

The Engineering About for...each and Collections

Taking a look in the MSIL for the for...each statement, we have a try... finally block and the .NET interface type System.IDisposable as part of the implementation of the enumerator returned for the System.Collections. ArrayList non-generic–based collection, and this is shown in Listing 4-11.

The MSIL generated by the compilers, whatever the programming language, can be complex code because the compilers generate a different sequence of intermediate code for debug, release, and a combination of compiling and linking options.

Listing 4-11 shows the parts that are more relevant for this explanation. The lines with source code in bold are the most relevant lines of code for you at this point of explanation.

Here is a list with the names of the variables and an explanation about each one of them:

- **string[] V_0** is the array used for a list of string values and the non-generic–based examples. The C# code is shown in Listing 4-1 with name values.

- **class [System.Runtime.Extensions]System.
  Collections.ArrayList V_2** is the non-generic–based
  collection. The C# code shown in Listing 4-1 is named
  nonGenericsList.

- **class [System.Runtime]System.Collections.
  IEnumerator V_8** is created automatically by the C#
  compiler to support the `for...each` statement and to
  store the enumerator instance returned by the instance of
  the non-generic–based collection, in this case, the .NET
  class type System.Collections.ArrayList non-generic base.

- **class [System.Runtime]System.IDisposable V_10** is
  created automatically by the C# compiler to support
  the `for...each` and the `try...finally` statements,
  and to store the enumerator instance returned by the
  instance of the non-generic–based collection with the
  implementation of the .NET interface type System.
  IDisposable, in this case, the .NET class type System.
  Collections.ArrayList non-generic base.

Listing 4-11. Excerpt of MSIL Generated by the C# Compiler and
the for...each Statement

```
.locals init (

        string[] V_0,

   uint32[] V_1,

        class [System.Runtime.Extensions]System.Collections.
        ArrayList V_2,

class [System.Runtime]System.Collections.IEnumerator V_4,
class [System.Runtime]System.Collections.Generic.
IEnumerator`1<uint32> V_5,
```

```
    class [System.Runtime]System.Collections.IEnumerator V_8,
    class [System.Runtime]System.IDisposable V_10,

)

IL_006d:   newobj      instance void [System.Runtime.
Extensions]System.Collections.ArrayList::.ctor()
IL_0072:   stloc.2
IL_0073:   ldloc.2
IL_0074:   ldloc.0
IL_0075:   callvirt    instance void [System.Runtime.
Extensions]System.Collections.ArrayList::AddRange(class
[System.Runtime]System.Collections.ICollection)
IL_0080:   stloc.3
IL_0081:   ldloc.3
IL_0082:   ldloc.1
IL_008a:   ldloc.2
IL_008b:   callvirt    instance class [System.Runtime]System.
Collections.IEnumerator [System.Runtime.Extensions]System.
Collections.ArrayList::GetEnumerator()
IL_0090:   stloc.s     V_8
.try
{
  IL_0092:   br.s        IL_00af
  IL_0094:   ldloc.s     V_8
  IL_0096:   callvirt    instance object [System.Runtime]
  System.Collections.IEnumerator::get_Current()
  IL_009b:   castclass   [System.Runtime]System.String
  IL_00a0:   stloc.s     V_9
  IL_00a2:   ldstr       "{0}\n"
  IL_00a7:   ldloc.s     V_9
```

```
IL_00a9:  call          void [System.Console]System.
Console::WriteLine(string, object)
IL_00af:  ldloc.s    V_8
IL_00b1:  callvirt    instance bool [System.Runtime]System.
Collections.IEnumerator::MoveNext()
IL_00b6:  brtrue.s    IL_0094
IL_00b8:  leave.s     IL_00d0
}  // end .try
finally
{
IL_00ba:  ldloc.s    V_8
IL_00bc:  isinst     [System.Runtime]System.IDisposable
IL_00c1:  stloc.s    V_10
IL_00c3:  ldloc.s    V_10
IL_00c5:  brfalse.s  IL_00cf
IL_00c7:  ldloc.s    V_10
IL_00c9:  callvirt    instance void [System.Runtime]System.
IDisposable::Dispose()
IL_00cf:  endfinally
}  // end handler
```

Listing 4-12 shows only the sequence of MSIL code that loads and stores in a variable of .NET interface type System.Collections.IEnumerator the reference to the instance of the enumerator returned by the instance of .NET class type System.Collections.ArrayList non-generic–based collections.

- **ldloc.2** is an MSIL instruction that loads the reference at the third (0,1,2) position in the stack for local variables. In this case, it is the instance of the System.Collections.ArrayList stored in the V_2 variable.

- **callvirt** is an MSIL instruction that calls the virtual method implementation of the System.Collections. ArrayList.GetEnumerator.

- **stloc.s V_8** is an MSIL instruction that stores in the variable V_8 (.NET interface type System.Collections. IEnumerator) the returned instance of the enumerator. This enumerator instance is returned by the virtual method implementation of the System.Collections. ArrayList.GetEnumerator.

Listing 4-12. MSIL Sequence That Loads and Stores the Instance of the Enumerator Returned by the System.Collections.ArrayList Non-Generic–Based Collection

```
IL_008a:  ldloc.2
IL_008b:  callvirt   instance class [System.Runtime]System.
Collections.IEnumerator [System.Runtime.Extensions]System.
Collections.ArrayList::GetEnumerator()
IL_0090:  stloc.s    V_8
```

Inside the try...finally block, specifically in the finally block, you have the following sequence of instructions, as shown in Listing 4-13:

- **ldloc.s V_8** loads the reference to the instance of the enumerator for the instance of the .NET class type System.Collections.ArrayList.

- **isinst [System.Runtime]System.IDisposable** verifies if the instance of the enumerator at V_8 has implemented the .NET interface type System.IDisposable.

- **stloc.s V_10** stores the reference to the instance for the enumerator returned by the instance method of.NET class type System.Collections.ArrayList.GetEnumerator.

- **ldloc.s V_10** loads the reference to the instance for the enumerator returned by the instance method of the .NET class type System.Collections.ArrayList. GetEnumerator.

Listing 4-13. MSIL Sequence with a Call for the System.IDisposable. Dispose Instance Method Implementation

```
.try
{
  IL_0092:  br.s       IL_00af
  IL_0094:  ldloc.s    V_8
  IL_0096:  callvirt   instance object [System.Runtime]
  System.Collections.IEnumerator::get_Current()
  IL_009b:  castclass  [System.Runtime]System.String
  IL_00a0:  stloc.s    V_9
  IL_00a2:  ldstr      "{0}\n"
  IL_00a7:  ldloc.s    V_9
  IL_00a9:  call       void [System.Console]System.
  Console::WriteLine(string, object)
  IL_00af:  ldloc.s    V_8
  IL_00b1:  callvirt   instance bool [System.Runtime]System.
  Collections.IEnumerator::MoveNext()
  IL_00b6:  brtrue.s   IL_0094
  IL_00b8:  leave.s    IL_00d0
} // end .try
finally
{
```

```
IL_00ba:    ldloc.s    V_8
IL_00bc:    isinst     [System.Runtime]System.IDisposable
IL_00c1:    stloc.s    V_10
IL_00c3:    ldloc.s    V_10
IL_00c5:    brfalse.s  IL_00cf
IL_00c7:    ldloc.s    V_10
IL_00c9:    callvirt   instance void [System.Runtime]System.
IDisposable::Dispose()
IL_00cf:    endfinally
}   // end handler
```

The reason for using the .NET interface type System.IDisposable is that the for...each statement in C# is checked by the compiler to see if the returned instance of the enumerator has implemented the .NET interface type System.IDisposable, and if true, the finally block is created following a sequence of rules described in the C# programming language specification, specifically about the for...each statement: https://docs.microsoft.com/en-us/dotnet/csharp/language-reference/language-specification/statements#the-foreach-statement.

The following blocks of explanations are based on excerpts of the C# specification about the for...each statement rules and the .NET interface type System.IDisposable implementation.

For example, if there is an implicit conversion from the instance of the enumerator to the .NET interface type System.IDisposable, and if the instance of the enumerator is a non-nullable, then the finally segment of the try...finally clause is expanded to the semantic equivalent of what is shown in Figure 4-32.

```
C#

finally {
    ((System.IDisposable)e).Dispose();
}
```

Figure 4-32. *Semantic equivalent in C# code that is generated when an implicit conversion of the instance of the enumerator for System. IDisposable is possible*

Otherwise, when an implicit conversion is not possible, in the `finally` segment of the `try...finally` clause, the C# code is expanded to the semantic equivalent of what is shown in Figure 4-33.

```
C#

finally {
    if (e != null) ((System.IDisposable)e).Dispose();
}
```

Figure 4-33. *Semantic equivalent in C# code that is generated when an implicit conversion of the instance of the enumerator for System. IDisposable is not possible*

Otherwise, if the instance of the enumerator is a sealed .NET type, in the `finally` segment of the `try...finally` clause, the C# code is expanded to an empty block, as shown in Figure 4-34.

```
C#

finally {
}
```

Figure 4-34. *Semantic equivalent in C# code that is generated when the .NET class type of the instance of the enumerator is sealed*

Otherwise, in the finally segment of the try...finally clause, the C# code is expanded to the semantic equivalent of what is shown in Figure 4-35.

```
C#

finally {
    System.IDisposable d = e as System.IDisposable;
    if (d != null) d.Dispose();
}
```

Figure 4-35. *Most common semantic equivalent in C# code that is generated*

Let's stop here for this chapter and continue with the explanations from this point in Chapter 5. In Chapter 5, I will start from the code for the generic part of the example using C# code and MSIL code. First, I will work in a review (or an introduction, if you have never worked with templates using the C++ programming language).

121

Summary

The next two sections offer recommendations about the uses of characteristics of .NET Core.

Dos

- Always check the Microsoft official repositories at `http://referencesource.microsoft.com` and `http://source.dot.net` to learn about the model used for the organization and behaviors of the .NET BCL/FCL types that the custom library is encapsulating.

- Avoid complex hierarchy for object models and implementation. Use .NET interface types and .NET class types from BCL and FCL as the starting points for complex object models, implementations, hierarchies, and then learn about implementations gradually.

Don't

- Ignore the knowledge available in the Microsoft official repositories at `http://referencesource.microsoft.com` and `http://source.dot.net`. You should learn about the model and behaviors used for the organization of the .NET BCL/FCL types that the custom library is encapsulating.

CHAPTER 5

Custom Collections - About C++ Templates and .NET Generics

In this chapter, I will continue to talk about fundamental aspects of implementing custom collections using the features and organization required for any .NET platform library implementation, but with a focus on generic technology.

When you work with collections, you follow patterns and standards, such as the behaviors you use to iterate through the instances of data types stored in an instance of a collection data type, non-generic or generic. Any .NET library implementation that is using collections is implementing patterns and following standards, which includes the required details for the .NET platform itself.

For example, every collection in the .NET libraries has a common set of base types that are required to be implemented and based on, such as the .NET interface type System.Collections.ICollection non-generic base and .NET interface type System.Collections.Generic.ICollection<T> generic base.

In this chapter, I'll use the .NET class type System.Collections.ArrayList non-generic base to explain the required .NET interface types for non-generic–based collections and the .NET class type System.Collections.Generic.List<T> generic base to explain the required .NET interface types for generic-based collections.

© Roger Villela 2020
R. Villela, *Understanding System.IO for .NET Core 3*,
https://doi.org/10.1007/978-1-4842-5872-9_5

These explanations and concepts are valid for any collection following the .NET standards for implementing .NET libraries, and for .NET Core, .NET Framework implementations, and respective libraries, BCL or FCL, or any others for .NET implementations.

Working with C++ Templates – Welcome, Everyone

One of the big points in a software development project is cost. In fact, this is a concern for any kind of project or action, for any area of human life, or in nature. But code offers another interesting area: that of *reuse*.

When working with .NET platform implementations and .NET libraries, we have a lot of reuse because we simply begin to write code and don't think in detail about things such as memory management, size of data structures, natural/non-natural alignment because of the size of words in the CPU register, the communication bus size between the memory and the CPU, and things like that.

One example is when working with .NET Windows Forms, which is the GUI framework (custom data types, custom libraries, and custom tools) based on Microsoft Windows GDI+ / Microsoft Windows GDI Windows APIs. Microsoft Windows GDI+ is written primarily using the C++ programming language, but with different programming techniques, including procedural programming, OOP, and specialized implementations.

Templates and Encapsulating Knowledge

The .NET Windows Forms encapsulates most of the technical details and aspects of programming directly with the Microsoft Windows GDI/GDI+ APIs, and for most of the time and for most tasks we don't have to think in detail about the management of the *Handle* object of a graphical *Window* object, allocation of a *heap* memory block to store certain informational items about the state of the graphical objects in use, and many others aspects that are required by a specialized graphical environment, as we have with Microsoft GDI/GDI+ or the more advanced graphical environment Microsoft DirectX, for example.

But encapsulate does not means hiding from us; simply put, it means that for one or more identified repetitive tasks it creates objects (data structures) with the behaviors (functions) that are a sequence of steps programmed for more flexible, efficient, and practical interactions with the callers and contexts.

For example, in Microsoft Windows GDI/GDI+ graphical environments and APIs, there is a "window" as a graphical item that is a fundamental concept and it has more than one data structure in the Microsoft Windows graphical APIs and subsystem that encapsulates information about the state of multiple graphical objects that are part of the window's graphical item context, such as one or more graphical icons, one or more text fonts, different sizes for object instances, and other specialized items.

Listing 5-1 and Listing 5-2 show declarations/definitions of the WNDCLASS window data structures of the WinUser.h header file that is part of the Microsoft Windows SDK header files. It is also installed with Microsoft Visual Studio 2019/Microsoft Visual C++ 2019.

The WNDCLASS window data structure has attributes with characteristics of a window object instance and has one implementation for ANSI and another implementation for Unicode support (wide) characters.

Listing 5-1. C++ Data Struct TagWNDCLASSA and WNDCLASSA, *PWNDCLASSA, *NPWNDCLASSA, and *LPWNDCLASSA Type Definitions for It

```
typedef struct tagWNDCLASSA {

    UINT        style;
    WNDPROC     lpfnWndProc;
```

```
    int           cbClsExtra;
    int           cbWndExtra;
    HINSTANCE     hInstance;
    HICON         hIcon;
    HCURSOR       hCursor;
    HBRUSH        hbrBackground;
    LPCSTR        lpszMenuName;
    LPCSTR        lpszClassName;

} WNDCLASSA, *PWNDCLASSA, NEAR *NPWNDCLASSA, FAR *LPWNDCLASSA;
```

Listing 5-2. C++ Data Struct TagWNDCLASSW and WNDCLASSW, *PWNDCLASSW, *NPWNDCLASSW, and *LPWNDCLASSW Type Definitions for It

```
typedef struct tagWNDCLASSW {

    UINT          style;
    WNDPROC       lpfnWndProc;
    int           cbClsExtra;
    int           cbWndExtra;
    HINSTANCE     hInstance;
    HICON         hIcon;
    HCURSOR       hCursor;
    HBRUSH        hbrBackground;
    LPCWSTR       lpszMenuName;
    LPCWSTR       lpszClassName;

} WNDCLASSW, *PWNDCLASSW, NEAR *NPWNDCLASSW, FAR *LPWNDCLASSW;
```

The WinUser.h header file contains a source code block right after the WNDCLASSA/ WNDCLASSAW type declarations/definitions, which is shown in Listing 5-3.

126

Listing 5-3. C++ Type Definitions WNDCLASS, PWNDCLASS, NPWNDCLASS, and LPWNDCLASS, respectively, for WNDCLASSW, PWNDCLASSW, NPWNDCLASSW, and LPWNDCLASSW When Using Support for the Unicode Standard, and WNDCLASSA, PWNDCLASSA, NPWNDCLASSA, and LPWNDCLASSA When Not Using the Support for the Unicode Standard

```
#ifdef UNICODE

typedef WNDCLASSW      WNDCLASS;
typedef PWNDCLASSW     PWNDCLASS;
typedef NPWNDCLASSW    NPWNDCLASS;
typedef LPWNDCLASSW    LPWNDCLASS;

#else

typedef WNDCLASSA      WNDCLASS;
typedef PWNDCLASSA     PWNDCLASS;
typedef NPWNDCLASSA    NPWNDCLASS;
typedef LPWNDCLASSA    LPWNDCLASS;

#endif // UNICODE
```

When working with Windows APIs and the C++ programming language for your source code base in your commercial projects, you are encouraged to use the WNDCLASS, PWNDCLASS, NPWNDCLASS, or LPWNDCLASS data types because you are creating levels of indirection and isolating the public APIs from the private and even more internal APIs and data structures of Microsoft Windows operating system features and of your own custom libraries.

This more abstract and less platform (software and hardware) dependent way of thinking helps a lot when designing, updating, correcting, removing, and adding APIs for your custom libraries for any context in software development, because you have data types and data

127

structures that encapsulate and implement levels of reuse for more private, internal data types and data structures that were not developed for direct exposure via one or more public APIs.

This is why you're not doing the one-by-one mapping of data types and data structures and development platforms as Microsoft Windows APIs and .NET libraries as a strategic plan, but just only eventual occurrences when transferring data between programming contexts, runtime contexts, or between "only" functions, to cite typical scenarios.

Fundamental Data Types

In Microsoft Windows APIs, this more abstract and less platform (software and hardware) dependent way of thinking is one of the pillars of the design and implementation, and it is applied even for most fundamental data types such as UINT that is a typedef for the unsigned int of C/C++ programming languages.

Listing 5-4 shows a UINT type definition for the unsigned int C/C++ fundamental data type. The UINT type definition is part of the minwindef.h header file that is part of the Microsoft Windows SDK header files for Microsoft Windows APIs.

Listing 5-4. UINT Type Definition for Unsigned int C/C++ Built-In Data Types and Others. All Part of the minwindef.h Header File

```
typedef unsigned int     UINT;

typedef int              INT;
typedef unsigned char    BYTE;
typedef unsigned short   WORD;
typedef float            FLOAT;
typedef unsigned long    DWORD;
```

The same principle is applied for keywords of C/C++ and assembly programming languages. For example, Listing 5-5 shows an excerpt of the minwindef.h header file for the definition of the CONST macro for the const keyword of the C/C++ programming languages.

Listing 5-5. An Excerpt of the minwindef.h Header File for the Definition of the CONST Macro for the const Keyword of the C/C++ Programming Languages

```
#ifndef CONST
#define CONST                const
#endif
```

The WNDCLASSA and WNDCLASSW data structures use LPCSTR and LPCWSTR, respectively. Both are defined in one of the most important public header files for every type of Microsoft Windows application or library: the WinNT.h header file. The WinNT.h header file is implicitly or explicitly included by other header files of Microsoft Windows APIs.

LPCSTR uses the CONST macro, which is defined in the minwindef.h header file, and the CHAR type definition that is part of the WinNT.h header file, as shown in Listing 5-6 with an excerpt of the WinNT.h header file.

Listing 5-6. C/C++ Type Definition of CHAR for C/C++ char Built-In Data Type

```
typedef char        CHAR;
```

Listing 5-7 shows the LPCSTR definition using the CONST macro part of the minwindef.h header file and the CHAR type definition part of the WinNT.h header file.

Listing 5-7. Type Definition for LPCSTR That Is Part of the WinNT.h Header File

```
typedef _Null_terminated_ CONST CHAR *LPCSTR, *PCSTR;
```

LPCWSTR also uses the CONST macro that is defined in the minwindef.h header file and the WCHAR type definition that is part of the WinNT.h header file, as shown in Listing 5-8 as an excerpt of the WinNT.h header file.

Listing 5-8. C/C++ Type Definition for WCHAR Windows API Data Type for C/C++ wchar_t Built-In Data Type in the WinNT.h Header File

```
#ifndef _MAC
typedef wchar_t WCHAR;     // wc,    16-bit UNICODE character
#else
// some Macintosh compilers don't define wchar_t in a
   convenient location, or define it as a char
typedef unsigned short WCHAR;     // wc,    16-bit UNICODE
                                           character
#endif
```

In the WinNT.h header file source code comments shown in Listing 5-8, you can see a block of text informing that some C/C++ compilers for the Apple platform do not put the definition for the wchar_t fundamental data type in a "convenient" location, or treat the wchar_t definition as the built-in data type char of the C/C++ programming languages.

Open the sample solution project <install_folder>\Sources\APIs\ Windows\WE-CPP\FundamentalTypes\wchar_t Type\wchar_t Type.sln that has the sample project wchar_t Type.

You must understand that wchar_t is a built-in data type defined by the C++ programming language standards and for the C++ programming language technological product. At the time of this writing, we do not have any wchar_t built-in data type as part of the C programming language standards for the C programming language technological product.

When the support for ISO C++ standard wchar_t was implemented as a built-in data type by the Microsoft C++ compiler and the C++ programming language, it was necessary differentiate C++ source code using wchar_t as a built-in data type and C++ source code using wchar_t as a type definition for unsigned short, another built-in C++ data type. For guaranteed compatibility with C++ source code created before the support for ISO C++ standard wchar_t built-in data type, "Treat WChar_t as Built in Type" was implemented by Microsoft C/C++ compilers, with the following options:

- **/Zc:wchar_t** that has the default value defined as on (active).

- **/Zc:wchar_t-** with the minus signed used together with the wchar_t keyword when off (deactivated).

The Microsoft C/C++ compilers have the /Zc (Conformance) compiler option with certain configurations available. You can check the full list of options through the Microsoft official documentation at https://docs.microsoft.com/en-us/cpp/build/reference/zc-conformance?view=vs-2019.

When using the /Zc:wchar_t default configuration, without the minus sign, and compiling a C++ source code, wchar_t is treated as a built-in data type in conformance with what is defined by the ISO C++ standard, and this is the default for the current implementation of the Microsoft C++ compiler for Microsoft Visual Studio 2019/Microsoft Visual C++, but this configuration is ignored when compiling C source code. You can disable the choice of conformance with the C++ standard using /Zc:wchar_t- (using the minus sign as part of the configuration option if you are compiling C source code).

Internally, Microsoft maps the wchar_t ISO C++ standard for the Microsoft-specific native and platform-specific __wchar_t. The wchar_t data type in the Microsoft compiler represents a 16-bit (two bytes) wide character used primarily for storing Unicode encoded in conformance with the UTF-16 Little-Endian (LE) standard specification, which is the native character type on Microsoft Windows operating systems.

Since UTF-16LE is the native character type on Microsoft Windows operating systems, the Microsoft UCRT and Windows API use wchar_t as a common data type for library functions, data types, parameters, and return values.

Figure 5-1 shows the configuration of a sample project.

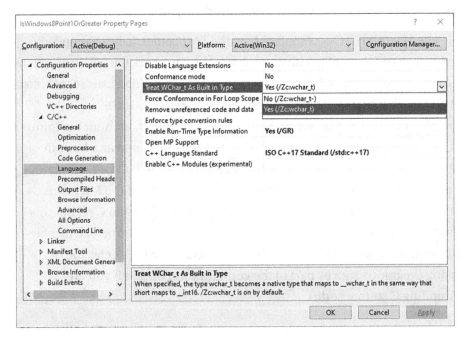

Figure 5-1. *"Treat WChar_t as Built in Type" was implemented by Microsoft C/C++ compilers, with the options /Zc:wchar_t that has the default value defined as on, and /Zc:wchar_t- with the minus signed used together with wchar_t keyword when off*

The Idea of a Template in Software Development Activities

The idea of a template in software development is to encapsulate and reuse knowledge, standards, concepts, algorithms, and source code. For example, if you have an algorithm that can be applied for arrays, independently of the base type of the items in the arrays, this algorithm can be a candidate for a template. You can implement a function algorithm using a template technology supported by the programming technology used in the C++ programming language, or the equivalent in .NET, which is the generic technology.

The C++ programming language has support for a technology called C++ Templates and the C++ Standard Library has functions and C++ data types that are based on the C++ Templates technology. The idea and implementation of the C++ Templates technology is not only for C++ classes or structs; it is applied to functions as well.

Let's start using an example of C++ Templates with functions of the C++ Standard Library. Open the solution `Templates.sln` in the `<install_folder>\` `CLR\System.IO\Ch05\` folder. Go to the Lesson00 C++ sample project with `wmain.cpp` as the principal source code file and a set of source code files with examples of the features and concepts of the C++ Templates technology.

At the time of this writing, you can check all the C++ Standard Library header files that have been implemented/supported/deprecated/removed by Microsoft Visual Studio 2019/Microsoft Visual C++ at this web page of the Microsoft official documentation: `https://docs.microsoft.com/en-us/cpp/` `standard-library/cpp-standard-library-header-files?view=vs-2019`.

The C++ Standard Library header files are organized by contexts (categories) such as

- Algorithms
- Atomic operations
- C Library wrappers
- Concepts
- Containers
- Sequence containers
- Ordered associative containers
- Unordered associative containers
- Container adaptors
- Container views
- Errors and exception handling
- General utilities
- I/O and formatting
- Iterators
- Language support
- Localization
- Math and numerics
- Memory management
- Multithreading
- Ranges
- Regular expressions
- Strings and character data
- Time
- ...

In the Lesson00 C++ sample project, open the `wmain.cpp`, `Arrays.cpp`, and `Arrays.h` source code files in the Microsoft Visual Studio 2019/Microsoft Visual C++ source code editor, as shown in Figure 5-2.

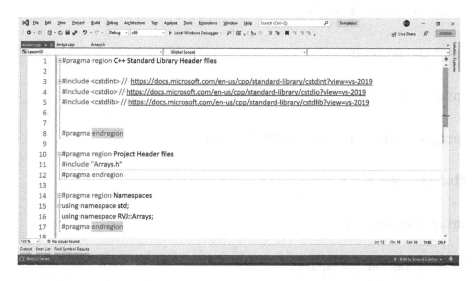

Figure 5-2. *The wmain.cpp C++ source code file of the Lesson00 sample project*

Listing 5-9 shows the C++ source code with the fundamental organization for the `wmain.cpp` source code file.

Listing 5-9. wmain.cpp C++ Source Code with the Fundamental Organization for the Source Code

```
#pragma region C++ Standard Library Header files

//  https://docs.microsoft.com/en-us/cpp/standard-library/
    cstdint?view=vs-2019

#include <cstdint>

//  https://docs.microsoft.com/en-us/cpp/standard-library/
    cstdio?view=vs-2019
```

```
#include <cstdio>

// https://docs.microsoft.com/en-us/cpp/standard-library/
   cstdlib?view=vs-2019

#include <cstdlib>

#pragma endregion

#pragma region Project Header file(s).

#include "Arrays.h"

#pragma endregion

#pragma region Namespaces

using namespace std;
using namespace RVJ::Arrays;

#pragma endregion

int32_t wmain( void ) {

        //int32_t _exitStatus = EXIT_FAILURE;
        int32_t _exitStatus = EXIT_SUCCESS;

        return _exitStatus;
};
```

The <cstdint>, <cstdio>, and <cstdlib> header files are part of the *C Library Wrappers* category of the C++ Standard Library.

Listing 5-10 shows the Arrays.h C++ header file that is part of the Lesson00 C++ sample project. It has declarations of the functions that are part of the namespace RVJ::Arrays.

Listing 5-10. The Arrays.h C++ Header File Has Declarations of the Functions That Are Part of the Namespace RVJ::Arrays

```
#pragma once

#pragma region C++ Standard Library Header files

// https://docs.microsoft.com/en-us/cpp/standard-library/
   cstdlib?view=vs-2019

#include <cstdlib>

// https://docs.microsoft.com/en-us/cpp/standard-library/
   cstdio?view=vs-2019

#include <cstdio>

// https://docs.microsoft.com/en-us/cpp/standard-library/
   array?view=vs-2019

#include <array>

#pragma endregion

#pragma region Namespaces
using namespace std;
#pragma endregion

extern "C++" namespace RVJ::Arrays {
```

```
template< typename _Type >
std::uint32_t IndexOf( _Type _element, std::uint32_t
_maxSize );
```

```
};
```

As shown in Listing 5-10, in the `Arrays.h` C++ header file you can see at the top of the file a region with the C++ header files that are included by the `Arrays.h` and that are part of the C++ Standard Library. The `<cstdlib>` and `<cstdio>` C++ header files are part of the category *C Library Wrappers* of the C++ Standard Library.

You also have the `<array>` C++ header file that is part of the category *Sequence Containers*, which is another category of C++ Standard Library. At the time of this writing, the *Sequence Containers* category has the following C++ header files:

- `<array>`
- `<deque>`
- `<forward_list>`
- `<list>`
- `<vector>`

The `<array>` and `<forward_list>` C++ header files were introduced in the C++ Standard Library as part of the C++11 Standard.

Listing 5-11 shows the `Arrays.cpp` C++ source code file content and the implementations for the functions declared in the `Arrays.h` C++ header file.

Listing 5-11. Arrays.cpp C++ Source Code File and the Implementations for the Functions Declared in the Arrays.h C++ Header File

```
#pragma region C++ Standard Library Header files
```

```cpp
// https://docs.microsoft.com/en-us/cpp/standard-library/
cstdint?view=vs-2019

#include <cstdint>

// https://docs.microsoft.com/en-us/cpp/standard-library/
   cstdio?view=vs-2019

#include <cstdio>

// https://docs.microsoft.com/en-us/cpp/standard-library/
   cstdlib?view=vs-2019

#include <cstdlib>

#pragma endregion

#pragma region Sample project header files

#include "Arrays.h"

#pragma endregion

#pragma region Namespaces

using namespace std;

#pragma endregion

namespace RVJ::Arrays {

template< typename _Type >
```

```
std::uint32_t IndexOf( _Type _element, std::uint32_t _maxSize )
{

    uint32_t _index{};

    // Implementation goes here...

    return _index;
};

};
```

The following page of the official documentation for Microsoft Visual C++ offers information about the idea of templates and their use in C++ programming languages: https://docs.microsoft.com/en-us/cpp/cpp/templates-cpp?view=vs-2019.

Returning to the wmain.cpp C++ source code file, as shown in Listing 5-12, you can see an example of the use of the std::array class template data type that is part of the *Sequence Containers* category of the C++ Standard Library. The purpose of the std::array class template data type is to enhance the characteristics of the typical concept associated with the traditional array, a fundamental data type supported by C++ programming language.

Listing 5-12. wmain.cpp and the Creation of an Instance of the std::array Class Template

```
#pragma region C++ Standard Library Header files

//  https://docs.microsoft.com/en-us/cpp/standard-library/
    cstdint?view=vs-2019

#include <cstdint>
```

```cpp
// https://docs.microsoft.com/en-us/cpp/standard-library/
   cstdio?view=vs-2019

#include <cstdio>

// https://docs.microsoft.com/en-us/cpp/standard-library/
   cstdlib?view=vs-2019

#include <cstdlib>

#pragma endregion

#pragma region Project Header files
#include "Arrays.h"
#pragma endregion

#pragma region Namespaces
using namespace std;
using namespace RVJ::Arrays;
#pragma endregion

int32_t wmain( void ) {

        //int32_t _exitStatus = EXIT_FAILURE;
        int32_t _exitStatus = EXIT_SUCCESS;

        constexpr uint32_t MaxSize{ 0x000Aui32 }; // Maximum
        number of elements in the instance of the array class
        template.

#pragma region Using array class template of C++ Standard
Library
```

```
    array<uint32_t, MaxSize> _numbers{ 0ui32, 1ui32, 2ui32,
    3ui32, 4ui32, 5ui32, 6ui32, 7ui32, 8ui32, 9ui32 };

#pragma endregion

    return _exitStatus;
};
```

The code in Listing 5-12 declares the _numbers variable as holding an instance using the std::array class template data type as the base type and informing two argument values for the template parameters of the std::array class template data type: the first is the base type of the elements, and the second is the total number of elements supported by the std::array instance. The std::array class template data type is defined in the <array> C++ header file that is part of the *Sequence Containers* category of the C++ Standard Library.

The std::array is named a *class template* for two obvious reasons. First, the data type array is declared as a class type data structure that is part of the C++ programming language supported resources for the object-oriented programming development techniques. Second, because the class type data structure is augmented with the support for the generic-programming capabilities through the C++ Templates technology.

In the array C++ source code file of the C++ Standard Library, the class keyword is used to declare the array class data type. The C++ Templates technology features are introduced to the type using the C++ programming language keywords template, and class or typename.

The class or typename C++ programming language keywords are used for the same purpose: introducing/declaring a placeholder type for a concrete type.

The class and typename C++ programming language keywords can be used interchangeably. But each development environment has specific cultural rules for coding, and individuals working in that professional field also have preferences for distinct reasons that should be considered and respected.

The std::array class template is declared using the C++ programming language keyword class instead of typename. The std::array class template has members, as does any other typical class data type of the C++ programming language, and your instance of std::array can access these members.

As a *class type,* it has members, but not only function members of the class template data type can be used with an instance of the class template data type.

There are function templates that are part of the various namespaces in the C++ Standard Library and other libraries, such as boost (www.boost.org), that can be applied for instances of class template data types, such as std::array class template data type.

Listing 5-13 shows a function template that is part of the std namespace, the std::sort() function template that can be applied to an instance of the std::array class template data type. Additionally, Listing 5-13 shows the use of two more member functions of the array class template data type, std::array::begin() and std::array::end(), used to get access to the first and last items of the sequence.

Listing 5-13. Two More Member Functions of the Array Class Template Data Types std::array::begin() and std::array::end(), Used to Get Access to the First and Last Items of the Sequence

```
#pragma region C++ Standard Library Header files

#include <cstdint> //  https://docs.microsoft.com/en-us/cpp/
standard-library/cstdint?view=vs-2019
#include <cstdio> // https://docs.microsoft.com/en-us/cpp/
standard-library/cstdio?view=vs-2019
#include <cstdlib> // https://docs.microsoft.com/en-us/cpp/
standard-library/cstdlib?view=vs-2019

#pragma endregion

#pragma region Project Header files
```

```
#include "Arrays.h"
#pragma endregion

#pragma region Namespaces
using namespace std;
using namespace RVJ::Arrays;
#pragma endregion

int32_t wmain( void ) {

        //int32_t _exitStatus = EXIT_FAILURE;
        int32_t _exitStatus = EXIT_SUCCESS;

        constexpr uint32_t MaxSize{ 0x000Aui32 }; // Maximum number
        of elements in the instance of the array class template.

#pragma region Using array class template data type of C++
Standard Library

        array<uint32_t, MaxSize> _numbers{ 0ui32, 1ui32, 2ui32,
        3ui32, 4ui32, 5ui32, 6ui32, 7ui32, 8ui32, 9ui32 };

        // Array of numbers unordered.
        array<uint32_t, MaxSize> _unorderedNumbers{ 9ui32, 8ui32,
        7ui32, 6ui32, 5ui32, 4ui32, 3ui32, 2ui32, 1ui32, 0ui32 };

        uint32_t _length{ _numbers.size() };

        std::sort( _unorderedNumbers.begin(), _unorderedNumbers.
        end() );

#pragma endregion

        return _exitStatus;
};
```

The idea, purpose, and implementation of the std::array::begin() and std::array::end() member functions are supported by the concept of an *iterator* used by *collections, containers, and similar data structures.*

In the .NET collections context, the general concept of an *iterator* in a C++ container or collection data types has a similar concept supported by the concepts and implementations of a .NET "Enumerable" and a .NET "Enumerator."

For example, for any .NET BCL implementation there is the .NET interface type System.Collections.IEnumerable for non-generic collections. One of the obligations of any .NET collection, non-generic or generic-based, is to **expose an enumerator, which supports a simple iteration over an instance of a collection.**

Based on collections patterns, as iterators, there is another very important feature in .NET for programming languages such as C#, Visual Basic, F#, and others, which supports the for...each pattern to iterate over instance items in an instance of a collection. The implementation of concepts and data types such as System.Collections.IEnumerable, System.Collections.IEnumerator, System.Collections.Generic.IEnumerable<T>, and System.Collections.Generic.IEnumerator<T> are required by the compilers and code generation technologies that the compilers are based on.

In the Microsoft official documentation for the C# programming language, the following web page with the title **Iterators(C#)** presents some of the fundamental aspects of collections and iterators, and that these concepts are part of the infrastructure of the .NET Libraries, such as .NET BCL, .NET FCL, or other specialized contexts, such as .NET Windows Forms, .NET WPF, and so on: https://docs.microsoft.com/en-us/dotnet/csharp/programming-guide/concepts/iterators.

Here is a list with links to the Microsoft official documentation website for .NET Framework and .NET Core web pages for the .NET BCL and .NET interface types System.Collections.IEnumerable and System.Collections.IEnumerator, non-generics and generics:

- **System.Collections.IEnumerable**

  - .NET Framework link: `https://docs.microsoft.com/en-us/dotnet/api/system.collections.ienumerable?view=netframework-4.8`

  - .NET Core link: `https://docs.microsoft.com/en-us/dotnet/api/system.collections.ienumerable?view=netcore-3.1`

- **System.Collections.IEnumerator**

  - .NET Framework link: `https://docs.microsoft.com/en-us/dotnet/api/system.collections.ienumerator?view=netframework-4.8`

  - .NET Core link: `https://docs.microsoft.com/en-us/dotnet/api/system.collections.ienumerator?view=netcore-3.1`

- **System.Collections.Generic.IEnumerable<T>**

  - .NET Framework link: `https://docs.microsoft.com/en-us/dotnet/api/system.collections.generic.ienumerable-1?view=netframework-4.8`

  - .NET Core link: `https://docs.microsoft.com/en-us/dotnet/api/system.collections.generic.ienumerable-1?view=netcore-3.1`

- **System.Collections.Generic.IEnumerator<T>**

  - .NET Framework link: `https://docs.microsoft.com/en-us/dotnet/api/system.collections.generic.ienumerator-1?view=netframework-4.8`

  - .NET Core link: `https://docs.microsoft.com/en-us/dotnet/api/system.collections.generic.ienumerator-1?view=netcore-3.1`

146

Let's return to the `wmain.cpp` source code file in your sample project Lesson00 of C++ Templates and the array class template implementation with the concept of an iterator. The implementation of the std::array::begin() and std::array::end() member functions are supported by the concept of an *iterator* in the following manner.

As you have with any collection that supports the concept of iterator, the concrete data types that have the implementations for acting as an iterator are not constructed to be exposed or used directly in APIs with public exposition.

Even when the iterator data type is public by the technical definition, used alone it is useless or has no contextual meaning without other data types with public or not public access. So, even when you find a data type with a public access, you should learn about the context before using the data type.

This means that is much easier to change details about the data type implementation of the iterator or even replace the data type with the role of iterator. For example, in .NET there is the idea of contract through the .NET interface type that is used as another level of indirection and isolation of implementation and that only exposes the members of the .NET interface and not the .NET type that implements the .NET interface contract.

In .NET BCL, every collection that offers support for a standard way to iterate over an instance of itself should implement System.Collections. IEnumerable for non-generic collections and should implement System. Collections.Generic.IEnumerable<T> for generic collections.

The System.Collections.IEnumerable.GetEnumerator() is the only method and returns an instance of type that implements the .NET interface System.Collections.IEnumerator.

The System.Collections.Generic.IEnumerable<T>.GetEnumerator() is the only method and returns an instance of type that implements the .NET interface System.Collections.Generic.IEnumerator<T>.

The "enumerator" is the implementation that iterates over the instance of the collection.

Figure 5-3 shows an excerpt of C# code for the implementation of the .NET class type System.Collections.Generic.List<T>.

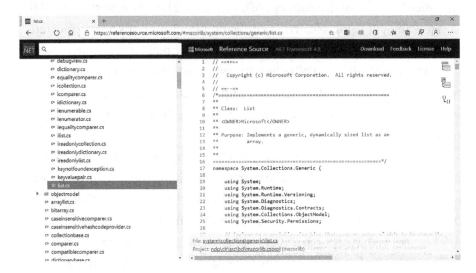

Figure 5-3. *The .NET class type System.Collections.Generic.List<T> is implemented using an array internally to store the elements*

As shown in Figure 5-4, one of the constructors of the System. Collections.Generic.List<T> has only one parameter and with System. Collections.Generic.IEnumerable<T> as the parameter type. This means that the argument value informed to the constructor must have implemented the .NET interface type System.Collections.Generic. IEnumerable<T>. Every type that has the System.Collections.Generic. IEnumerable<T> implemented must have one or more partner data types acting as the enumerator for that collection data type.

Figure 5-4. *One of the constructors of the System.Collections. Generic.List<T> has a parameter with System.Collections.Generic. IEnumerable<T> as the base type. (Microsoft Source Code of List.cs)*

Figure 5-5 shows an excerpt of the source code of the constructor that has a parameter type System.Collections.Generic.IEnumerable<T>. The block of code is assuming that the System.Collections.Generic. IEnumerable<T>.GetEnumerator() method implementation is returning a valid instance for an enumerator from the instance of the data type informed as the argument value for the constructor's parameter.

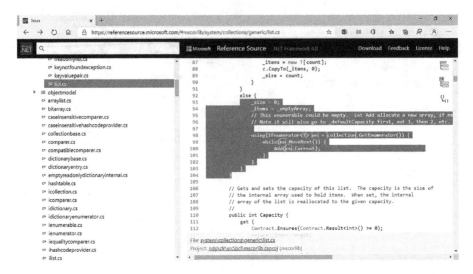

Figure 5-5. *The implementation is using the instance of System. Collections.Generic.IEnumerator<T> of the argument value informed to the constructor*

Figure 5-6 shows another block of the `List.cs` source code file, and it has the implementation of the System.Collections.Generic.List<T>. GetEnumerator() method because System.Collections.Generic.List<T> has declared the .NET interface type System.Collections.Generic. IEnumerable<T> as one of base .NET types.

The implementation of the System.Collections.Generic.List<T>. GetEnumerator() method returns an instance of a value type, not a reference type. This value type has the name Enumerator.

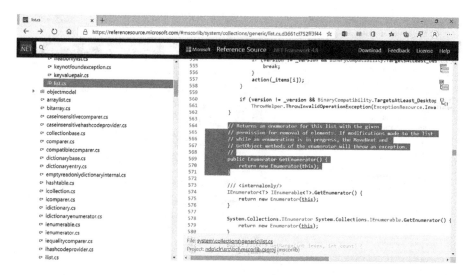

Figure 5-6. *The method is returning an instance of a .NET value type, not a .NET reference type. This .NET value type has the name Enumerator*

The Enumerator is a .NET value type declared inside the List.cs source code file and has System.Collections.Generic.IEnumerator<T> and System.Collections.IEnumerator as the base .NET interface data types. This is shown in Figure 5-7.

With all the required interfaces implemented, when you are using them in your source code for an application, you don't have the names of the enumerator's data types of the .NET collections' data types, with generic support or without generic support. Internally, the .NET collections are much less restricted about changes or replacements of data types because these more specialized data types, as in the scenarios with the enumerators' data types, were not created to be exposed through public APIs.

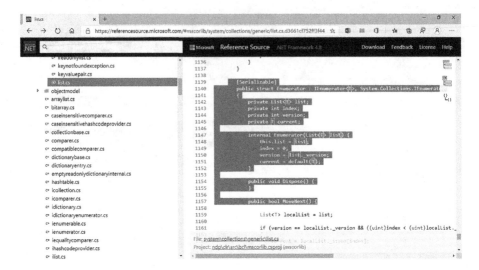

Figure 5-7. *The Enumerator is a .NET value type declared inside the List.cs source code file and has System.Collections.Generic. IEnumerator<T> and System.Collections.IEnumerator as the base .NET interface data types*

The point here is a common aspect for the .NET types: a set of .NET interface types are related based on inheritance between contracts. That is, instead of a .NET class type declared with multiple .NET interface types at the class level, the .NET class type is declared with few .NET interface types, but they are composed of a succession of .NET interface types that, in the final, create the full expected collection type with the required behaviors and concepts available.

Let's stop here for this chapter and continue with the explanations from this point in Chapters 6. In Chapter 6, I will start from code for the generic part of the example using the C# code and the MSIL code. Then I will talk about unmanaged code, unmanaged data types, the .NET, and the System.IO unmanaged data types.

CHAPTER 6

Unmanaged .NET Data Types and System.IO

In this chapter, you will learn about the fundamental aspects of implementing the features and organization required for any .NET platform library implementations, but with a focus on unmanaged code and unmanaged data types, the .NET and the System.IO unmanaged data types.

Unmanaged .NET Data Types and System.IO

The .NET data types in System.IO and the other namespaces of System.IO have specialized data types for interacting with System.IO.Ports, System.IO.Pipes, System.IO.MemoryMappedFiles, and others, and use the collections and the patterns and concepts that are the base of all .NET collections.

Figure 6-1 shows the following assemblies:

- mscorlib.dll

- netstandard.dll

- System.IO.UnmanagedMemoryStream.dll

- System.Runtime.InteropServices.dll

© Roger Villela 2020
R. Villela, *Understanding System.IO for .NET Core 3*,
https://doi.org/10.1007/978-1-4842-5872-9_6

The System.IO.UnmanagedMemoryStream .NET reference type is not CLS-compliant; remember that the CLS is part of the ECMA-335 specification and is a set of rules intended to promote programming language interoperability. In order to conform to the CLS, these rules must be followed.

But a non-CLS compliant .NET data type is still valid from the perspective of the CLR and the .NET platform. The point here is that the non-CLS compliant .NET data type was not created to guarantee support for the multiple programming languages' characteristics in .NET because the support of multiple programming languages should require, for example, restrictions on the use of certain features, or multiple implementations of the same type for achieving requirements of different compilers and programming languages.

UnmanagedMemoryStream Class

Namespace: System.IO

Assemblies: System.IO.UnmanagedMemoryStream.dll, mscorlib.dll, netstandard.dll,
System.Runtime.InteropServices.dll

Important

This API is not CLS-compliant.

Figure 6-1. *A non-CLS compliant .NET data type is still valid from the perspective of the CLR and the .NET platform*

When working with unmanaged .NET data types, the implementation of the System.IDisposable .NET interface data type is one typical element in unmanaged .NET data types.

The implementation of the System.IDisposable interface .NET data type is a pattern adopted by .NET BCL and .NET FCL, and it is recommended or required for custom libraries for .NET platform.

"Recommended" means that, if you are not using certain language-specific shortcuts, like the "using" construct for the C# programming language or the "Using" construct for the Visual Basic .NET programming language, which expects the System.IDisposable .NET interface data type implemented by the .NET data type included in the language construction, you are not required to implement the interface.

"Required" means that scenarios, such as the "using" construct for C# programming language or the "Using" construct for Visual Basic .NET programming language, the for...each pattern, and the use of unmanaged .NET data types, expect the use of System.IDisposable as a fundamental pattern and implementation practice, and not to be ignored by the implementers.

The System.IO.UnmanagedMemoryStream unmanaged .NET data type has two methods named Dispose(); one is the implementation of System.IDisposable.Dispose() and the other is that of the .NET data type itself.

The Microsoft official documentation has an observation about that scenario of using System.IDisposable interface .NET data type, as shown in Figure 6-2.

> ⓘ **Note**
>
> This type implements the **IDisposable** interface, but does not actually have any resources to dispose. This means that disposing it by directly calling **Dispose()** or by using a language construct such as `using` (in C#) or `Using` (in Visual Basic) is not necessary.

Figure 6-2. *The usage and implementation scenarios of System. IDisposable is not applied in the same way for specialized types in System.IO and interoperability between managed and unmanaged code*

Figure 6-3 shows the source code of the System. IO.UnmanagedMemoryStream unmanaged .NET data type from the Microsoft official reference source website, and Figure 6-4 shows the source code from Microsoft official repository for .NET Core.

Figure 6-3. *The System.IO.UnmanagedMemoryStream unmanaged .NET data type is derived from System.IO.Stream, which implements the System.IDisposable interface .NET data type. This model is followed by .NET Framework BCL and .NET Core BCL*

Figure 6-4. *The fundamental model followed by the .NET Framework BCL and .NET Core BCL implementations of the System. IO.UnmanagedMemoryStream unmanaged .NET data is the same*

The System.IO.UnmanagedMemoryStream unmanaged .NET data type is derived from System.IO.Stream, which implements the System. IDisposable interface .NET data type, as shown in Figure 6-5 for .NET Framework and in Figure 6-6 for .NET Core.

For .NET Framework and .NET Core, the System.IO.Stream .NET data type is declared and defined as an abstract .NET data type and has System. IDisposable as part of the declaration and implementation of non-abstract members, as shown in Figure 6-5 for .NET Framework and in Figure 6-6 for .NET Core.

Figure 6-5. *For .NET Framework and .NET Core, the System. IO.Stream .NET data type can be defined with different supported features and base types*

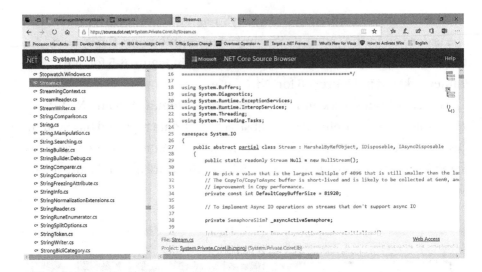

Figure 6-6. *The .NET Core System.IO.Stream .NET data type is defined with different supported features and base types, such as the support for .NET Async as part of specialized interface IAsyncDisposable for release of unmanaged resources*

For the implementation of the System.IO.Stream.Dispose(System. Boolean) method, a typical member of the .NET data type is created to be implicitly inherited and visible by descendants because it is defined as protected, and overridable because it is defined as virtual.

For the implementation of the System.IO.Stream.Dispose(void) method that is the implementation of System.IDisposable interface .NET data type member, it's defined as public, meaning that any other .NET type can call it directly via an instance of a descendant of the System.IO.Stream .NET data type.

The implementations of Dispose() methods for the .NET Framework and .NET Core are the same. As shown in Figure 6-8 and Figure 6-9, the implementation of the System.IDisposable.Dispose() method calls the System. IO.Stream.Close() method, and the final cleanup of unmanaged resources is realized in the System.IO.Stream.Close() method, instead of the System. IDisposable.Dispose() method, as expected by the pattern. This is the reason behind the note in the Microsoft official documentation, warning that by the actual implementation calling the Dispose() method is not required.

This is not a small question, and in the source code with the implementation of the System.IO.Stream.Close() method, you can see lines of comments about this scenario with the implementation of System. IDisposable, as shown in Figure 6-7.

```
// Stream used to require that all cleanup logic went into Close(),
// which was thought up before we invented IDisposable.  However, we
// need to follow the IDisposable pattern so that users can write
// sensible subclasses without needing to inspect all their base
// classes, and without worrying about version brittleness, from a
// base class switching to the Dispose pattern.  We're moving
// Stream to the Dispose(bool) pattern - that's where all subclasses
// should put their cleanup starting in V2.
public virtual void Close()
{
    /* These are correct, but we'd have to fix PipeStream & NetworkStream very carefully.
    Contract.Ensures(CanRead == false);
    Contract.Ensures(CanWrite == false);
    Contract.Ensures(CanSeek == false);
    */

    Dispose(true);
    GC.SuppressFinalize(this);
}
```

Figure 6-7.   *The soure code contains lines of comments about this scenario with the implementation of System.IDisposable and the importance of the Dispose pattern*

The purpose of these lines of comments is that at some point in a future work of re-engineering, the release of unmanaged resources will be realized following the Dispose pattern, as describe by the ECMA-335 official specification for the .NET platform and shown in Figure 6-8 and Figure 6-9.

Figure 6-8. *Excerpt of .NET Framework BCL source code showing the implementation of the System.IDisposable.Dispose() method, which calls the System.IO.Stream.Close() method, and the final cleanup of unmanaged resources realized in System.IO.Stream.Close() instead of System.IDisposable.Dispose(), as expected by the pattern*

Figure 6-9. *The .NET Core BCL implementation of System. IDisposable.Dispose() method calls the System.IO.Stream.Close() method, and the final cleanup of unmanaged resources is realized in System.IO.Stream.Close() instead of System.IDisposable.Dispose(), as expected by the pattern*

In the System.IO.UnmanagedMemoryStream .NET data type, the inherited implementation of System.IO.Stream.Dispose(System.Boolean) is overridden, and that implementation is made in that way to be called immediately and to avoid the possible delay with the GC mechanisms and the typical behavior associated with the implementation and System.IDisposable, which is recognized by the GC mechanisms and others CLR mechanisms.

Figure 6-10 and Figure 6-11 show the implementations for the System. IO.UnmanagedMemoryStream .NET data type for .NET Framework and .NET Core, respectively.

```
[System.Security.SecuritySafeCritical]  // auto-generated
protected override void Dispose(bool disposing)
{
    _isOpen = false;
    unsafe { _mem = null; }

    // Stream allocates WaitHandles for async calls. So for correctness
    // call base.Dispose(disposing) for better perf, avoiding waiting
    // for the finalizers to run on those types.
    base.Dispose(disposing);
}
```

Figure 6-10. *The overriden implementation of System.IO.Stream in System.IO.UnmanagedMemoryStream for .NET Framework BCL*

```
/// <summary>
/// Closes the stream. The stream's memory needs to be dealt with separately.
/// </summary>
/// <param name="disposing"></param>
protected override void Dispose(bool disposing)
{
    _isOpen = false;
    unsafe { _mem = null; }

    base.Dispose(disposing);
}
```

Figure 6-11. *The overriden implementation of System.IO.Stream in System.IO.UnmanagedMemoryStream for .NET Core BCL*

System.IO.UnmanagedMemoryStream .NET Data Type As an Example

Listing 6-1 and Listing 6-2 show a sample class that encapsulates the functionalities of System.IO.UnmanagedMemoryStream and a console application as the client that uses this sample class.

The project, source files, .NET data type, or the member of the .NET data type should be explicitly configured for the support of unsafe operations, as shown in Figure 6-12 in the case of project configuration.

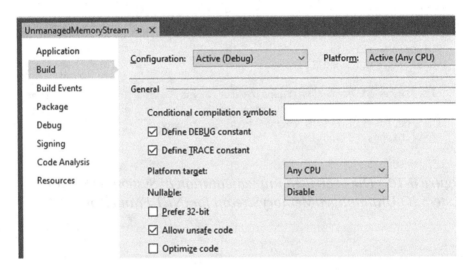

Figure 6-12. *The project, source files, .NET data type, or the member of .NET data type should be explicitly configured for the support of unsafe operations*

Listing 6-1. The Custom .NET Data Type RVJ.UnmanagedMemory

```
#region Namespaces
using System;
using System.IO;
using System.Text;
```

```
using System.Runtime.InteropServices;
#endregion

namespace RVJ {
    public unsafe class UnmanagedMemory : System.Object {

        #region Private members
        private String _localBuffer = null;
        private System.IO.UnmanagedMemoryStream _
        unmanagedStream = null;
        private Int32 _bufferSizeInBytes;
        private IntPtr _memoryBlock;
        #endregion

        #region Constructors
        public UnmanagedMemory() : base() {
            return;
        }

        public UnmanagedMemory( String value ) : this() {

            this._localBuffer = value;

            return;
        }
        #endregion

        #region Closes the unmanaged memory stream.
        public void Close() {

            Marshal.FreeHGlobal( this._memoryBlock );
            this._unmanagedStream.Close();

            return;
        }
        #endregion
```

```
#region Read a sequence of instances of System.Byte
from a memory block using an unmanaged stream .
public void ReadAll( out Byte[] _buffer ) {

    _buffer = new Byte[ this._bufferSizeInBytes ];

    this._unmanagedStream.Position = 0;
    this._unmanagedStream.Read( _buffer, 0,
    this._bufferSizeInBytes );

    return;
}
#endregion

#region Write a sequence of instances of System.Byte in
a memory block using an unmanaged stream .
public void WriteAll() {

    if ( ( this._localBuffer != null ) &&
    ( this._localBuffer.Length > 0 ) ) {

        this._bufferSizeInBytes = UnicodeEncoding.
        Unicode.GetByteCount( this._localBuffer );

        this._memoryBlock = Marshal.AllocHGlobal(
        this._bufferSizeInBytes );

        this._unmanagedStream = new System.
        IO.UnmanagedMemoryStream( ( ( Byte* )
        this._memoryBlock.ToPointer() ), this._
        bufferSizeInBytes, this._bufferSizeInBytes,
        FileAccess.ReadWrite );

        this._unmanagedStream.Write( UnicodeEncoding.
        Unicode.GetBytes( this._localBuffer ) );
```

```
        };

        return;
    }
    #endregion
};
};
```

Highlighted in Listing 6-1 are some important points that are part of any unmanaged code, and not only for this scenario. When interacting with unmanaged code, the .NET BCL, .NET FCL, and the CLR itself provide a set of specialized technologies and .NET data types for this context of development and interaction between managed and unmanaged code.

In general, you should not try to "reinvent" something for System.IO namespaces using C/C++ programming languages and integrate it in System. IO via P/Invoke if you don't have an objective and technical reason to do it.

As example, consider the System.Runtime.InteropServices.dll assembly. Note that mscorlib.dll and netstandard.dll also have specialized .NET data types for required tasks when working with unmanaged code.

The System.Runtime.InteropServices.Marshal is a .NET reference type defined as static, and it provides methods for operations with unmanaged memory such as allocation, copying, converting between managed and unmanaged types, and more.

Listing 6-2. Client Console Application Using the RVJ. UnmanagedMemory .NET Data Type

```
#region Namespaces
using System;
using System.Text;
#endregion
```

```
namespace RVJ {
    public class Program : System.Object {
        public static void Main() {

            String _sampleMessage = "Unmanaged .NET data
            types";
            Byte[] _localBuffer;

            RVJ.UnmanagedMemory _unmanagedMemory = new RVJ.
            UnmanagedMemory( _sampleMessage );

            _unmanagedMemory.WriteAll();
            _unmanagedMemory.ReadAll( out _localBuffer );
            _unmanagedMemory.Close();

            _ = UnicodeEncoding.Unicode.GetString( _localBuffer );

            return;
        }
    };
};
```

When working with unmanaged .NET data types, by default, your
code is in charge of allocating and deallocating the blocks of unmanaged
memory. The System.IO.UnmanagedMemoryStream unmanaged
.NET data type that you are using as an example does not have any
implemented logic for automatically allocating and deallocating the
unmanaged memory. In the sample project, you are using System.
Runtime.InteropServices.Marshal.AllocHGlobal() and System.Runtime.
InteropServices.Marshal.FreeHGlobal() to allocate and deallocate blocks
of unmanaged memory.

When writing code using the System.IO .NET data types,
which internally use unmanaged code as you can see with System.
IO.UnmanagedMemoryStream as example, you must be aware that the

native APIs used internally are different on different operating systems. System.Runtime.InteropServices.Marshal.AllocHGlobal() and System. Runtime.InteropServices.Marshal.FreeHGlobal() for Microsoft Windows use the native Windows API, and functions such as LocalAlloc() and LocalFree() and the Unix-based implementation use specialized APIs such as CRT-based or others specific to the operating system environment.

Another important aspect when using unmanaged APIs is that not every interaction between managed environment and the native APIs are supported by the different implementations of .NET. The System.Runtime. InteropServices.Marshal.ReadByte() method is supported by the current implementations of the .NET Framework BCL and .NET Core BCL, but in the Mono .NET Core source code for `Marshal.cs`, the method is not supported, as shown in Listing 6-3.

Listing 6-3. For Unmanaged Code and .NET Data Types, Not Every Method Is Supported by All .NET platform Implementations. The Mono .NET Core Source Code for Marshal.cs Contains Examples

```
using System.Reflection;
using System.Runtime.CompilerServices;

namespace System.Runtime.InteropServices {
    public partial class Marshal {

        public static byte ReadByte( object ptr, int ofs ) {
            // Obsolete
            throw new PlatformNotSupportedException();
        }

        public static short ReadInt16( object ptr, int ofs ) {
            // Obsolete
            throw new PlatformNotSupportedException();
        }
```

```
public static int ReadInt32( object ptr, int ofs ) {
    // Obsolete
    throw new PlatformNotSupportedException();
}

public static long ReadInt64( object ptr, int ofs ) {
    // Obsolete
    throw new PlatformNotSupportedException();
}

public static void WriteByte( object ptr, int ofs,
byte val ) {
    // Obsolete
    throw new PlatformNotSupportedException();
}
    };
};
```

Another interesting scenario when talking about cross-platform issues and the Mono implementation of .NET is the definition of the System.Runtime.InteropServices.Marshal.AllocHGlobal() and System.Runtime.InteropServices.Marshal.FreeHGlobal() methods, as shown in Figure 6-13. These and other methods have the attribute System.Runtime.CompilerServices.MethodImplAttribute .NET data type with the enum value of MethodImplOptions.InternalCall defining that the native function APIs used for these specialized scenarios are part of each implementation of the CLR and certain components, such as the virtual machine for each target platform.

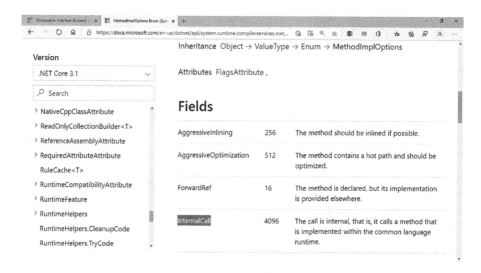

Figure 6-13. *Specialized scenarios are part of each implementation of the CLR and certain components, such as the virtual machine for each target platform*

Index

A

Architecture and implementation
  BCL System.IO, 26
  characteristics (.NET Core),
      52–55
  conditional compilation
      symbols, 30–32
  data types, 29–30
  encapsulation (*see*
      Encapsulation data types)
  high-level view, 26–27
  namespaces, 25–26, 28
  official documentation page,
      28–30
  reference type, 28
  support libraries (internal), 27
  technological contexts, 26–27

B

Base Class Library (BCL), 3, 80

C

C++/CLI projection
  blog posts, 73
  CLR class library, 73–74
  CLR properties page, 75–76
  folder configurations, 74
  future of, 73
  project/advance properties
      page, 75
  source code, 76–77
C++ Standard Library
  Arrays.h C++ header file, 137
  class /typename, 142–143
  fundamental organization,
      135–136
  generic-programming, 142
  header files, 133–134
  object-oriented
      programming, 142
  sequence containers, 138
  source code editor, 135
C++ templates and .NET generics
  data encapsulation, 124–128
  fundamental data type, 128–132
  library implementation, 123
  minwindef.h header
      file, 128
  reuse libraries, 124
  software development
      (*see* Software development
      activities)
  WinNT.h header file, 130
  WNDCLASS data structure, 125

© Roger Villela 2020
R. Villela, *Understanding System.IO for .NET Core 3*,
https://doi.org/10.1007/978-1-4842-5872-9

Collections
    base data types, 79
    characteristics (.NET Core), 122
    features, 79
    for...each statement, 113–121
    generic base type, 86–94
    generic technology (*see* C++
        templates and .NET
        generics)
    iterate (*see* Iteration)
    non-generic data type, 80–86
    patterns/standards, 79
Common Language Runtime
    (CLR), 73–76

D

Data types
    BCL System.IO
        namespace, 58–59
    characteristics (.NET Core),
        77–78
    encapsulation of, 57
    enum implementation, 58
    ILDASM tool, 58–59
    internal structure, 63
    MSIL implementation, 64, 65
    RVJ.IO.FileMode, 62
    streams (*see* Stream data types)
    System.Enum
        declaration, 57–58, 64
    System.IO.DriveType, 58
    System.IO.FileAccess enum, 61
    value members, 60

E

Encapsulation data types
    data type StreamInformation,
        39–47
    data stream types, 38–40
    functionalities, 35
    RVJ.IO custom data types, 33
    RVJ.IO.FileMode, 35–37
    RVJ.IO.IStream Interface, 48–50
    RVJ.IO.IStreamInformation
        Interface, 50–52
    RVJ.IO.StreamType, 38
    System.IO.DriveType, 34–35
Enumerator pattern
    class type implementation,
        109–111
    code declaration, 107–108
    concept/pattern, 107
    for...each and collections, 113–121
    generic type, 108
    instance method, 110–111
    MoveNext() method, 109
    .NET interface type, 107–112
    non-generic type, 107–109
    Reset() method, 109
    semantic equivalent, 120–121
    try... finally block, 117
Extensible Application Markup
    Language (XAML), 4

F, G, H

Framework Class Library (FCL), 3

I, J, K, L, M

IEnumerable<T> and IEnumerable
    interfaces
    code declaration, 103–107
    constructors, 100–101
    generic type, 104–106
    instance method, 102–103
    IntelliSense, 101–102
    .NET interface type, 103–107
    non-generic type, 104–106
    parameter data type, 101–103
Iteration
    collection data type, 95–96
    constructor signature, 98
    enum (*see* Enumerator pattern)
    for...each pattern, 95–96
    generic-based type, 94–95
    IEnumerable<T> and
        IEnumerable interfaces,
        100–107
    instance method, 99
    IntelliSense code, 99
    statement/programming
        language, 96–98

N, O, P, Q

.NET Core and projects
    acronyms, 1–2
    ASP.NET Core platform, 4
    BCL/FCL, 3
    characteristics of, 22–24, 52–55
    data types (*see* System.IO
        unmanaged data types)

GitHub repository, 2–3
    official repository, 4
    open source project, 2
    repositories, 2
    runtime/framework, 2
    UI frameworks, 4–5
Non-generic/generic-based, 145

R

RVJ.IO library creation runtime
    architecture and implementation
        (*see* Architecture and
        implementation)
    class library project, 11–12
    .csproj project file, 13–15
    debug tab, 13
    name/path configurations, 12
    .NET Standard 2.1 configuration
        file, 15–17
    project templates, 8–10
    start window, 10
    target framework, 17–22
    XML tags, 14

S

Software development activities
    C++ (*see* C++ Standard Library)
    concepts/data types, 145
    constructors, 148–149
    enumerator, 152
    file/implementations, 138–140
    function template, 143–144

Software development
activities (*cont.*)
iteration, 145
List.cs source code file, 150
.NET class type, 148
non-generic/generic-based
type, 145
programming technology, 133
returning method, 151
System.Collections.Generic.
IEnumerator<T>, 150
System.Collections.
IEnumerable, 145
System.Collections.
IEnumerator, 146
wmain.cpp file, 140–142
Stream data types
class declaration, 66–68
IFileInformation.cs, 72–73
IStreamInformation public
interface, 68–72
IStream public interface, 68–72
projects/source code, 66
reference type, 67–68
RVJ.IO.IStreamInformation,
72–73
System.IO unmanaged data types
assemblies, 153
BCL source code/
implementation, 160
Dispose() methods, 158
fundamental model, 156
namespaces, 153
non-CLS compliant, 154

overriden implementation, 161
source code, 155
System.IDisposable
interface, 155, 159
System.IO.Stream.Dispose()
method, 158
System.IO.Unmanaged
MemoryStream
client console application,
165–166
console application, 162
Marshal.cs file, 167–168
source code, 162–165
specialized scenarios,
168–169
unsafe operations, 162

T, U, V, W, X, Y, Z

Target Framework Moniker (TFM)
chronogram, 7
conditional symbols
core, 21
framework, 20
RVJ.IO source code, 22
standard, 21
.csproj project file, 8
netcore451/netcore45, 18
netcoreapp, 17
netstandard, 18
project file, 19
project file
format/application, 5–8
uap10.0, 18

Printed in the United States
By Bookmasters